995

THE GOOD LIFE◀

Fabiola Cabeza de Baca Gilbert ◀

Drawings By Gerri Chandler ◀

▸THE
▸GOOD
▸LIFE

▸ New Mexico
▸ Traditions and Food

▸ Museum of New Mexico Press

All new materials copyright © 1982
The Museum of New Mexico Press
Post Office Box 2087, Santa Fe, New Mexico 87503

FIRST EDITION: 1949
SECOND EDITION: 1982
SECOND PRINTING, SECOND EDITION: 1986

ISBN: 0-89013-137-6
Library of Congress Catalog Card Number 81-83160

Designed by Merle Armitage

10 9 8 7 6 5 4 3

▶ PREFACE

The recipes which are a part of *The Good Life* and the family traditions from which the recipes have developed have been a part of my life. They have been a part of the lives of Hispanic New Mexicans since the Spanish colonization of New Mexico.

I was reared on the family ranch at La Liendre, south of Las Vegas. My mother died when I was four and my brother, two sisters and I were reared by my paternal grandmother, Estefanita Delgado C. de Baca, and my father, Don Graciano C. de Baca. It was on this New Mexico ranch, by my grandmother's side in her home at La Liendre and outdoors by my father's side, that I began to experience "the good life."

I began teaching in the rural schools of Guadalupe County in 1915 while intermittently attending New Mexico Normal, now New Mexico Highlands University. I studied one year at Centro de Estudios Historicos in Madrid, Spain, and returned to Highlands in 1921 to receive my baccalaureate degree in pedagogy. After further teaching in New Mexico schools I entered New Mexico College of Agriculture and Mechanic Arts, now New Mexico State University, and graduated from there as a home economist in 1929. As a home economist I began my long work among the people of the northern New Mexico villages which continued until my retirement in 1959.

Life as I grew up and as I knew it as a home economist was rich but simple. People drew their sustenance from the soil and from the spirit. Life was good, but not always easy. There were crop failures resulting from nature's unpredictable ways; there were family concerns, despair alternating with hope. Faith was deep, though, and having faith could bring the hope of better things — a hope for life that was good.

This simple story of the Turrieta family, the family in *The*

Good Life, revolves around the observances and traditions of what could have been any Hispanic family in a New Mexico village during that period of my work as a home economist. The same pattern of life is followed today in many isolated New Mexico villages. The foods are those I knew as a child in my grandmother's home. The recipes for them have been passed down in New Mexico households for generations, often adapted to conditions and to the availability of certain ingredients of the locale. As a home economist/nutritionist I tested the recipes in the homes of the people with whom I worked and in the kitchen laboratory of my own home. The recipes in the book have, of course, been changed from "un poquito de...y un poquito de..." to more workable measures. Otherwise, they are the same as those used by our Spanish forebears and those adopted from their Indian friends.

The fondest memories of my life are associated with the people among whom I have worked. The ways of life expressed in the book and the recipes which are a part of those lives have helped make for me *The Good Life.* As you use the recipes I hope you will think of my people and the occasions in the lives of those people who added "un poquito de...y un poquito de..." to produce savorous and nutritious New Mexico foods.

Fabiola Cabeza de Baca Gilbert
Santa Fe, New Mexico
November, 1981

CONTENTS ◀

▶ INTRODUCTION

Old sayings, proverbs and old wives' tales unlike old coins seem never to lose face, no matter how often or how badly they may be used. "The way to a man's heart" et cetera, et cetera, a saying as true today as when first coined is one of them, and the importance of this search is proved by the countless cookbooks that, since printing was first discovered, have been and still are being produced.

So far as I know we have not yet discovered among the pictographs and petroglyphs which decorate the sandstone cliffs and dislodged boulders in our Southwest, the particular glyph which tells how to make the piki bread and the pemmican used by those pre-Spanish, pre-Anglo picture writers. But I am sure they must be there. Who knows for instance, whether the crudely drawn circles so commonly found on our cliffs, styled by the archaeologists the "sun symbol," might not in truth be a picture of the first *tortilla* patted out by the brown hands of one of our early Basket Maker housewives? Who is there to say?

Of the making of cook books there is no end. Nor will there be until the demand for food and its preparation (not to include the before mentioned heart), come to an end. Cook books there are in all languages and all lands, telling the how and the why of

1

preparing all edible foods, vegetable and animal. Most of these are to be had in English translations, making them available to American housewives and the latest cooking converts, their husbands.

On my own kitchen shelf there is an old English cook book, no date, but of sufficient age to give directions on the preparation and cooking of game birds before we had progressed far enough esthetically to discard the "innerds," *any* of them! together with the good English beef roast, kidney stew, the thick mutton chop and sustaining English muffins.

There is a French book, untranslated, giving directions for making delectable sauces which accompany most dishes, and proclaim the French Chef. Beside it stands an Oriental cook book telling the best way to concoct a pilaf, the staff of the Oriental dinner and a delicious addition to any menu. A Chinese cook book gives explicit directions for cooking eel in a net, steamed turtle, boned duck leaving it whole for serving, shark fins, fish swimming in a golden pond, food of the God of Law Horn, Immortal food which is said to prolong life beyond the century mark. But there is no receipe for chop suey!

A Belgian cook book companions the Chinese, written the preface says, "not for the millionaire but for the common man who must watch his purse strings." Savories say the Belgians "Must be like the ankle, small, neat and alluring." Also they declare in the same foreword, "The perfect cook, like Miss 'Arris or the fourth dimension is never found." Hence the necessity for the cook book.

Traveling about the world sampling its foods my kitchen cook book shelf comes back to our own land with 200 YEARS OF CHARLESTOWN COOKING, THE BREAD TRAY, with nearly six hundred ways of making bread. Beside all these on the shelf stands also Erna Fergusson's NEW MEXICO COOKERY, and a vacant space for THE GOOD LIFE. But for all these cook books my best recipes are those left me by my Mother and my Grandmother.

With all this telling of foods and how to prepare them there is no clear telling of the people who consume them, of their ways of life or their philosophies. Some one has said, "Tell me what a man eats and I'll tell you what he is." But only by the use of one's imag-

2

ination projected through the various nations can cook books picture the people or their every day lives. This leaves much to be desired. But now in THE GOOD LIFE for the first time so far as I know, this need is met. For this is not only a cook book, it is also a folklore book with this added interest, value and flavor. The family around which the book is written is an old family, living in an isolated village, carrying on the traditions of the early Spanish colonizers, living the life as it was in those days among the early New Mexicans of Spanish and Indian extraction.

In a straightforward and entertaining manner THE GOOD LIFE brings the fascinating life of the Conquistadores from the dim past into the every day light of now.

The food of those early days being limited in variety by the lack of diversity in agriculture, conditioned as it was by the exigencies of life, climate, and soil, of necessity lacked variety. This lack must be met and a varied diet achieved by differing the methods of preparation, in order that the appetite might not pall. This situation naturally developed the ingenuity of the housemother who devised the many different ways of preparing the simple foods then to be had: jerky, beans, corn and chili.

Of course, in those days there were no corner groceries, no friendly markets where canned goods or frozen foods could be found. The entire year's supply was grown upon the small patch of land belonging to the householder, who in order to meet the needs of the winter diet must dry such summer foods as meats, corn, squashes and fruits as were available. For all the lack of variety, however, there was little lack in nutrition. A diet of chili, beans, corn and jerky being approved today as a balanced diet.

There is no more delicious way to prepare green corn than any of the several ways derived from the Indian. Roast green corn, steamed dried corn, corn tamales, corn with green chili, as well as our New England corn on the cob, also derived from the Indian. In many ways we of today have lost much in losing the simply prepared staple foods of the American colonial days, the primitive days of our history.

Together with the foods used and its preparation THE GOOD LIFE brings to light the year round life of the people of the New

3

Kingdom and their customs which in the years following the conquest have all but disappeared in the populous areas where modern customs have taken their place. But in the more isolated villages of New Mexico families are to be found who still cling to the Colonial ways of life, preserving among the older members the customs of Spanish Colonial days, with life on the hacienda.

THE GOOD LIFE is a book to read and enjoy as well as a cook book to follow in the preparation of New Mexican foods.

In speaking of her book the author says: "As a home economist I am happy to see modern kitchens and improved diets, but my artistic soul deplores the passing of beautiful customs which in spite of New Mexico's isolation in the past, gave us happiness and abundant living."

In this I heartily agree and recommend THE GOOD LIFE.

Ina Sizer Cassidy

AUTUMN HARVEST

1

The short summer months in northern New Mexico had gone by like a gust of wind. Here was fall in full splendor. Apples hung from trees in red clusters and the plum trees were loaded with green and purple fruit. It was the time for harvest in El Alamo and the farm folks were busy.

The red and orange coloring of the trees and shrubs seemed to give everyone new courage. Fall, the time of plenty with its seasoned hues, brings hope to those who toil, because in it they see the reward of their labors.

On the patio of the Turrieta home lay piles of red peppers ready to be made into strings. Two days of sun had cured the pods and they were now ready to be made into *ristras,* the lovely red strings one sees drying in the sun as one travels through the New Mexico villages in the fall.

Doña Paula gave her family an early supper in readiness for the neighbors who were coming in to help make the strings. The store room had been cleared for the job and Don Teodoro was busy filling the oil lamps before the first helpers arrived.

Doña Refugio García and her family were the first ones to come; then came Doña Petra with her husband, Don José, and their two sons. After greetings were exchanged, the army of laborers started on their work.

Men, women and children joined in the task. Each one, seated on the ground, deftly started tying the pods. Tilano, the goat herder and story teller, stood at the door waiting for his chance to get in a word.

Doña Paula who had been watching him from the corner of her eye spoke to him, "Good evening Tilano. Come in, there is a lovely pile waiting for you too." Tilano did not like to do anything which exerted his strength so he merely sat down, took a chew of tobacco and watched silently while the others worked. He knew the audience were anxiously waiting for him to start a piece of gossip so that they could expand on it.

As he spit out a stream of tobacco juice, he started,

"What is happening in the village, are we all going to join the *Aleluyas?*"

Doña Refugio without raising her head and tying chile pods as fast as her fingers could move, answered,

"Do you think we all have lost our minds? Don't you know that we already have a religion?"

Doña Paula joined in saying,

"We have a good religion we do not need to seek another. Our faith has guided us through many bad years. God has seen that we do not want."

"Yes," chimed in Don Teodoro, "We thought that we would not have enough water to see us through this year and now look at the beautiful chile piled here. Has God not been good to us? Why should we forsake the teachings of the church which has guided us through the years?"

Tilano with bowed head replied, "The *Aleluyas* say that there is no future in being a Roman Catholic and they told me that if I

6

joined them I would not have to herd goats for you for such low wages, Don Teodoro."

"What do they offer you in place of herding goats, Tilano?" asked Don Teodoro.

"They didn't say, but I think I shall try the *Aleluyas*. I like their singing with the guitar accompaniment and I could play for them."

"Why don't you play the guitar for us Tilano," said Doña Paula. "Go into the *sala,* the living room, the guitar is hanging in there."

Tilano did not need coaxing. No sooner had Doña Paula spoken than Tilano was playing familiar strains. Some of the young folks joined in by singing which made Tilano so happy that he forgot the *Aleluyas*.

The work went on for hours and as soon as enough pods had been tied, Doña Petra and Don José started braiding them. How well they did their jobs. As they worked they talked; they talked about their crops and what they had yet to do. The next evening they would all gather at Doña Refugio's to help with her strings.

At midnight, Doña Paula went into the kitchen and soon the aroma of freshly boiled coffee reached the tired folk.

"Wash your hands and come into the kitchen to have a cup of coffee," called Doña Paula from inside.

The table with its clean flowered oil cloth was carefully laid for the guests and the Turrieta family. As they took their places for the repast they looked so tired, so worn and bent — young and old. The coffee, and the *buñuelos,* the freshly fried bread, seemed to put new life into them.

Don Teodoro, the gracious host, made sure that everyone was properly served with sugar and goat's milk in their coffee. Doña Paula had the milk piping hot to give the coffee the right flavor.

One by one the neighbors departed with *muy buenas noches* meaning good night and *hasta mañana,* hoping to meet on the morrow.

Before day-break Doña Paula and Don Teodoro were eating breakfast. As they ate Doña Paula said,

"These children of ours will starve on farming. They sleep until the sun is in the middle of the sky."

"It is your fault," replied Don Teodoro. "My mother made us

get up at dawn. When we heard her entone the hymn '*Ya viene el alba, ya viene el día, Cantemos todos Ave María,*' we jumped out of bed and answered by repeating after her,

> 'Daylight breaks
> Dawn is here
> Let us all sing
> Ave Maria.'"

"Yes in our day we had respect for our parents, but now we are too easy on our children," said Doña Paula and in the same breath continued,

"We have five sacks of green chile to roast and peel before the day is over and although there is a lot of work involved, how good it will taste to us next winter when we cannot go out in the garden to pick it fresh."

Don Teodoro, before breakfast, had built a big wood fire in the outdoor mud oven in order to have plenty of coals for the roasting of the peppers.

On the patio sat Doña Paula clipping the end of each pod to keep it from bursting with the heat and before the oven was hot, she had all the peppers ready for roasting. The wood in the oven soon turned into bright red coals which made it just right for blistering the skins.

Doña Paula took a basketful of the chile and emptied it into the coals. With a stick she carefully turned the peppers until they were browned on all sides; then she took them out, put them into a pan, sprinkled them with water and covered them. This was done so that the peppers would steam and make them easier to peel. The oven was quickly filled each time it was emptied, keeping Doña Paula busy all morning.

Although the family had been up since dawn, yet every minute counted towards finishing the day's tasks.

"While the chile is steaming," commanded Doña Paula to her children, "Go to the field and pick red peppers. Frost will be here before we know it and with you in school, I shall be left with all the work."

In less than an hour, a batch of roasted peppers were ready and

8

the job of peeling occupied every member of the family except Don Teodoro and José. They were out in the field cutting green corn for drying.

How skillfully the women went at their task of peeling chile without a pod being torn by their agile fingers. While her daughters, María, Rosa and Cuca peeled peppers, Doña Paula strung the pods by the stems; when she had a string three feet long, she went to the yard and hung it from a line. The green strings blended beautifully with the red ones which Don Teodoro had hung out in the early morning.

Everytime the oven was emptied, it was replenished by a new supply of peppers, keeping the women busy all day. Doña Paula stopped occasionally, but just long enough to put a stick of wood in the kitchen stove for the beans to be ready for the noon day meal.

That morning before her children were up, Doña Paula had made a cheese from goat's milk.

Cheese making was as regular a chore as bread making. Tilano had brought in the milk and before it got cold Doña Paula had put in two tablespoons of liquid rennet into each pail. (She always saved the rennet when a kid or goat was butchered and each day she added whey to it to keep it alive.) It took about half an hour for the milk to coagulate. Doña Paula then broke the curd with her hand and she removed as much of the whey as possible; while she went about preparing breakfast, she had let the curd stand. When the whey and curd had separated, Doña Paula, in an improvised mold cut from a coffee can, had placed the drained curd and molded it with her hands into a beautiful white cheese.

As the sun climbed up in the sky, the early risers began to feel the pangs of hunger and with the odor of roasting chile the gastric juices began to flow freely. Doña Paula, who well knew when her family was hungry, took a pan full of roasted peppers and went into the kitchen and soon the odor of freshly cooking *tortillas,* the flat bread which she cooked on top of the stove, reached the workers out in the yard. The beans had been cooking in the Indian earthenware pot since early morning.

Don Teodoro must have smelled the food, for he was on his way towards the house when Doña Paula called,

"Dinner is ready. Cuca, call your father and José."

A happy family sat down for their noonday meal. Every morsel of food had come from their land and that made Don Teodoro very proud.

Don Teodoro had news to relate and had anxiously waited for the moment. Everybody was silent as Don Teodoro spoke to his wife.

"José wishes us to ask Comadre Refugio for her daughter's hand in marriage."

"Which one of the daughters," asked Doña Paula.

"As if you did not know," he replied smiling.

Tears trickled down Doña Paula's cheeks as she thought of her José growing up and starting a family of his own.

Wiping her tears she said,

"Panchita is a very good girl. The García family comes from excellent stock. We could not wish anyone better for our son."

José blushed but said nothing. He was thinking of Panchita. How lovely she had seemed the evening before as she strung the chile peppers. The red of the chile seemed to match her black hair. Her milky white hands had moved so fast and José wondered if they would ever be brown and wrinkled like Doña Refugio's.

"We have no time for weddings just now," said Don Teodoro. "We can think of that after we have finished the harvest. Now, José, start digging the hole for the corn. Panchita may be watching from her window so it better be a masterpiece. Comadre Refugio demands much of those who enter her household."

A pile of corn was waiting to be husked. Don Teodoro and José who had been in the corn field all morning had brought three wagon loads of corn which would supply the family with *chicos,* the dried steamed corn. They could even sell a bushel or two to Don Nolasco.

José obeying his father started digging a hole near the pile of corn.

Don Teodoro and four of his neighbors were removing husks from the ears of corn leaving only those needed to hold in the steam while the corn roasted.

The hole which José dug measured six feet across and three feet deep. After it was ready, he built a fire in it and as soon as the

10

wood had turned into coals he covered it with an iron lid held fast by rocks. He then helped with the husking.

When the sun was about to sink behind the mountains, the corn was ready to go into the hole which José had prepared. Carefully, Don Teodoro sprinkled the ears of corn with water while José removed the coals and neatly placed each ear; he then covered it as he had done before, making sure that no heat would escape during the night.

The women had finished with the peeling of the chile and Doña Paula was calling her family to supper. The smell of roasting kid was all over the place. In the middle of the table was a pile of beautiful round *tortillas,* a bowl of green chile and another one with homemade butter which Doña Paula had just made.

That morning she had skimmed the evening's milk and saved the thick cream which she beat with a spoon until it turned into yellow butter to spread on the flat round bread.

The dishes were quickly cleared and the Turrieta family walked over to Doña Refugio's farm. The sun had not yet gone down and as they were on their way Doña Paula remarked, "Comadre Refugio always makes the most of the help, so it is well to go early. No wonder she has made money when the rest of us have barely kept body and soul together."

Don Teodoro responded by saying, "It takes much labor to make a living from our small acreage. One must never sleep and Comadre Refugio knows the secret."

Tilano was heard driving the goats into the corral. He made as much noise as if a dozen goatherders were putting the goats in for the night. He enjoyed the neighborly gatherings as the only entertainment in his simple life, and he was hurrying the goats so as not to miss any of the gossip.

By morning the corn was ready to come out of the pit in which it had lain all night. Doña Paula and Don Teodoro were turning back the husks and hanging the ears to dry before the rest of the family began to stir. Doña Paula knew that the corn had steamed enough but she tried each ear by pinching it with her fingernails. It was a matter of years of habit.

Don Teodoro loved to watch his wife at work. She moved so

11

fast. Her long black gathered skirt sewed to a band seemed always to sag at the waist line. Her blouse with the usual round collar was well tucked in her skirt; on her head she wore a blue bandana folded in triangle shape, the point coming at the nape of her neck. How lovely she had been as a girl! Her hair had been golden like the ears of corn which were hanging on the line stretched between two poles, but at forty her hair was streaked with gray and as with all children of the soil had lost its golden hue and turned brown. Her skin which had been pink like a rose petal was wrinkled and tanned. The blue of her eyes had not changed but was intensified by the darkness of her skin. Her hands were rough and wrinkled, yet they were lovely, because they had been useful.

When the children were in evidence around the house, Don Teodoro turned to his wife and said,

"We are going into Santa Fé today. This is the day the dentist said he would finish pulling your teeth. You want to make a good showing for our son's wedding."

"Most likely," answered Doña Paula, "I shall never get used to those artificial inventions. It was a whim of my modern daughters that I get a new set of teeth. When I was a girl, I took it as natural for an old woman to lose her teeth and do nothing about it."

"Now, now," said Don Teodoro. "You know that you are as vain as your daughters. Get ready, Don Nolasco waits for no one. His truck will be here before you get your skirts tied on."

"Must we always go with Don Nolasco? He bleeds us in his store and we must pay him to take us in his truck. I know it will be filled before he gets here and we shall go bouncing in the back getting the full benefit of the wind," murmured Doña Paula.

"He has the truck, my dear. We have no choice," calmly replied Don Teodoro.

In less than one could count ten, Doña Paula had put on her black silk dress and on her head she wore a black hat with red flowers.

THE HERB WOMAN
2

The next morning, as Doña Paula was preparing summer squash for drying, Señá Martina came by with a sack full of herbs. She had been out in the fields since dawn gathering medicinal herbs which she shared with her neighbors. Señá Martina was the *curandera,* the medicine woman of the village. Very often she went out to neighboring towns to heal persons from various maladies and her fame as a medicine woman stretched over many miles.

After greeting Doña Paula she sat down beside her and without being asked, she took over the task of slicing small squashes into circles in preparation for drying.

Doña Paula became curious to know if Señá Martina had discovered any new herbs.

"What did you bring me today?" she inquired.

"The usual remedies," she replied. "You need a new supply this year.

"Shall I spread them out to dry for you?" she asked as she reached for her sack.

Doña Paula went into the kitchen to get some string while Señá Martina spread out her herbs on the patio. She sorted the plants in neat piles ready for tying.

The medicine woman seemed so old and wrinkled to Doña Paula and she wondered how old she was. No one remembered when she was born. She had been a slave in the García family for two generations and that was all any one knew. She had not wanted her freedom, yet she had always been free. She had never married, but she had several sons and daughters. Doña Paula had heard many tales about Señá Martina. Some said the children belonged to the *patrón*, the master, under whom she had worked; others said they were his grandchildren. Doña Paula thought, "What right have I thinking of such things? They are children of God and they have been good sons and daughters. That is all that matters."

"Señá Martina, you will have to tell me the names of the plants and what their uses are. I can never remember from one year to another," said Doña Paula.

"You young people believe too much in doctors and you have no faith in plants," answered Señá Martina as she picked up a bunch of plants and tied them.

"When I was young, there were no doctors and we lived through many sicknesses.

"Children died from the evil eye because no one can compete with the devil, but they did not die from colic. Here is some *manzanilla*, camomile from my garden. A strong tea brewed from it cures the colic. It is always well to rub the stomach of the ailing child with camphorized fat and to keep him from eating solid food. A gruel made from wheat flour with a little sugar and anise seed helps to stop the diarrhea.

"Doña Paula, why don't you put down all the prescriptions that I give you each year? You who can write need not rely on your memory only, as I have for years. I cannot live forever and when I am gone you will have no one to ask."

"You are right," said Doña Paula. "I shall write them down." She had said the same thing for twenty years. But she kept on slicing squash.

Señá Martina sorting out herbs took a bunch of elder-berry

14

flowers. "These," she said, "cannot fail to ease a fever and it is also a pleasant tea to drink. You should have a bush in your yard."

"Yes, of course," answered Doña Paula, "I have been telling José to bring a cutting from your garden."

"I brought you some dry rose petals, because with all your many tasks, I knew you would forget to gather some. Crushed rose petals mixed with powdered alum are the best remedy for sore gums.

"I did not see any *azafrán,* saffron, in your garden this year and I know you will need it for seasoning. Do you remember when your children had the measles? You thought it was only a cold. When I gave them saffron tea, the measles broke out at once. The *curandera* knows a few things."

"Thank God for you, Señá Martina," said Doña Paula. "You have been an angel of mercy in our village for two generations and yet we do not appreciate you enough. We take you for granted."

Señá Martina did not seem to hear. She kept on sorting her herbs.

"This was a good year for *poleo,* pennyroyal, and I gathered bushels of it along the ditches. If the doctor tells you your children have tonsilitis don't let him cut the tonsils as everyone is doing; mix pulverized pennyroyal leaves with butter and rub the white spots in their throats. Take my word, they will not need a knife. It is even good for diptheria."

"Diptheria is contagious Señá Martina. It is better to let the doctor treat that."

"Be as you say — but I cured all my children without assistance from a doctor which I could not have afforded, anyway.

"When Juanito, my youngest, came down with it, I was all the doctor he had. Every night I rubbed him with camphorized whiskey to bring a good sweat and his throat soon healed with the pennyroyal and butter paste. Today he is as well as any one can be, although deaf, he is a healthy man.

"I dug out *canaigre* roots last evening which are so good for sore gums and loose teeth. They will tighten if you chew on the *canaigre* roots and if I had practiced medicine on myself, I would have all my teeth instead of only these two which you see. So would you, but you believe the dentist more than you do me."

Doña Paula wondered if Señá Martina were not right; but her

daughters and Don Teodoro saw to it that she went to the dentist in town. She merely said, "We have to keep up with the times."

"Not with the times, Doña Paula, with your neighbors, or they will laugh at you. They have laughed at me, but I am too old to care so I laugh at them too.

"When the doctor cannot do anything for them, they come to me, then I laugh inside of me.

"Last year Doña Refugio, who does not believe in my remedies, swallowed her pride and came to me with your future daughter-in-law. Her flux had stopped for over two months and the doctor could not bring it on. I did. Each night for nine days, I made her sit on a hot bath of strong *yerba de la víbora,* snake brush, in which I had dropped nine rounded stones. On the ninth day there it was. It was only a cold in her insides."

"You know too much, Señá Martina. What are these roots here?"

"This is *inmortal,* spider milkweed. Grated and snuffed up into the nostrils cures nose catarrh and the grated powder dissolved in water is also good for nausea, stomach ache and for heart ailments.

"This is *contrahierba,* dorstenia contrayerba, which grated and dissolved in water can be used as an antidote for almost any poison and it is also good for the evil eye. When boiled until thick it serves as a tonic to build up the blood. This tonic is also the best known remedy to produce sweating.

"And this is *oshá,* wild mountain parsnip. You know, you should never let your children go out to the fields without a piece in their pockets. Its odor keeps poisonous snakes away. Grated and put into diluted whiskey cures a cold quicker than all the doctors' medicines.

"I brought you some *cáscara de capulín,* choke cherry bark. I noticed you spinning some wool last year and I thought perhaps you would like to dye with it as we did for my masters. It produces a beautiful red and the *chamiza* here is for yellow. The *canaigre,* which you have already, is for brown. There are many others that can be used for dyeing, but I am more interested in the medicinal power of plants.

"Here is some *waco,* bee weed, which we Indians, like to eat as greens, but it also makes a good tea for diarrhea and colic."

"How do you cook *waco* to take the bitterness out of it?" asked Doña Paula.

16

"That is simple. The secret is in using a metal kettle in which to cook it, but if you do not have a copper or iron vessel, drop a nail or a metal spoon into whatever container you use and the bitterness will be absorbed by the metal.

"For sores and ulcers, I brought you some *castilleja,* beard tongue. Stupes made from it and applied soon heals them. I just found a few wild onion tops this year and I knew that you would need some; keep them well covered, so that they will not lose their strength and use them as smelling salts for fainting spells.

"Did you gather *chimajá,* wild parsley, last spring? I had the rheumatism so bad after the cold winter that I did not go out in the hills."

"Yes, we brought some," answered Doña Paula. "I like it for flavoring fresh peas and also for dried pea soup. I have wanted to ask you, how do you prepare it for greens?"

Señá Martina thought for a while as its use for food was quickly disappearing and she had almost forgotten.

"Wash the tops carefully, place a layer of them in a pan, sprinkle with salt and dot with fat; place another layer and proceed as before. Cover with clean corn husks then sprinkle with water and place in the oven to cook. It takes a very short time to cook, not any longer than other greens which are cooked in steam on top of the stove."

"What is good for rheumatism?" asked Doña Paula. "Don Teodoro had such a spell of it last winter."

"There is nothing better than baths with snake brush. Boil it well and take a bath in it as hot as you can stand it. I would not be walking today if I had not done that for the last twenty years.

"It is getting late and you have supper to get, so I must be going," said Señá Martina.

"But there are still more herbs you have not told me about in that neat pile there."

"These are getting so scarce that I only brought you a few leaves; the men pull them up as weeds.

"Here is some *mariola,* rubber bush, which is so good for bringing down a fever. And this is *hediondilla,* creosote, to use for baths when there is high fever.

"Your girls will like some *poñil,* Apache plume, for washing their hair; it gives it lustre and keeps it from falling out. I did not bring them *yerba de la negrita,* bristly mallow, this year, it is time they do it themselves. It will make their hair grow and there is nothing better for scalp irritations.

"I brought you some *mastranzo,* round leaved mint, from my garden, for poisonous insect bites; it kills aphids in plants too. This *estafiate,* wormwood, came from Doña Refugio's place; it cures severe headaches — just chew on it. Made into a tea, it has no equal for all stomach disorders.

"I hope to live another year, for when I am gone my remedies go with me and the doctors will get fat from your generosity.

"I did not gather *coto,* galium, and if the girls want some they can gather their own supply; the tea is good to drink and it cures stomach ulcers.

"I saw fields of *malvas,* common mallow, in your back yard. You can pick them yourself for I am getting too old and you might as well get used to doing it now. *Malva* stupes are a cure for all kinds of infections.

"And don't forget to have Don Teodoro bring some *amole,* yucca roots, when he goes after wood. The ladies in my day had beautiful hair but only because *amole* suds can make it so."

Señá Martina shook her apron, tied on her blue bandana and showed intentions of leaving as she said,

"It is late and I must go, now. Next time that I come, I shall bring you some hand brooms. I have not had time to clean them and they are sure beauties this year."

"Have a cup of chocolate before you go," called Doña Paula from the kitchen.

The sack which Señá Martina had brought with herbs was resting by the kitchen door. It was full again. As she looked at it, she said,

"You should not have done that, Doña Paula."

They were only idle words for she knew that her herbs would not let her go hungry. She boasted that the relief workers had never had to come to her house.

18

WINTER'S PLENTY

3

CANE MOLASSES

The days were getting colder and snow could already be seen in the high mountain peaks, but the farm folks were still busy with the harvesting of crops. Although neighbors helped each other, the short autumn days seemed to vanish more rapidly than the really short winter days when their farm work was done.

Don Teodoro and José ate their breakfast by lamplight while Tilano hitched the horses to the wagon which was to bring the sugar cane to the press to be ground. Their small subsistence acreage had not allowed them to plant much cane but there was enough to turn into molasses for the family table. On the day before, Don Teodoro and José had cut the cane with a sickle and now they were bringing it to the yard of their house where the cane mill stood.

José unhitched the horses from the wagon and hitched one to the pole that controlled the lever which turned the cane mill. Don

19

Teodoro fed the stalks to the rollers which were set on a block and as José drove the horse, the rollers ground the cane and extracted the juice. A trough made from two boards extended from the mill frame and this served to carry the juice into a large kettle. As soon as one container filled up, Tilano took it to Doña Paula who was waiting to strain it into the copper kettle which was used for making the molasses. The shed where the kettle rested had a roof made from pine logs. The sides were open with only a small adobe wall about two feet high around it which served as a stand to hold the kettle under which the fire was built. At one end there was a smokestack built of adobe also and this allowed the smoke to come out while the molasses cooked.

Doña Paula put in just enough strained juice at one time in the kettle so that it would not boil over. In order to avoid a green taste, she added a little water. As the molasses boiled, a green scum came to the top and Doña Paula carefully skimmed it until no more green appeared; she then let it cook to the thickness and color desired. She preferred a golden brown for general use, but she also let some get dark brown and thick in order to please Scñá Martina who liked it for making sweet rolls.

The molasses was put in barrels in the store room and what was left, Doña Paula bottled for immediate use.

PINON PICKING

The autumn chores were finished in El Alamo. This was a piñón year and the Turrieta family had not yet put in their winter's supply.

As the family sat by the fireside Doña Paula said,

"We must go to bed early tonight and those of you who are not ready by the time the coffee starts boiling in the morning will not go piñón picking; if we do not get an early start we shall lose the day."

It seemed that they had hardly gone to bed when the aroma of freshly made coffee reached those who were still in bed.

Don Teodoro had prepared the wagon the night before. Tilano

sleepily was helping him hitch the team, while the others were snatching a hasty breakfast. Doña Paula with skirts flying, moved fast getting the house put in order and the lunch ready.

They had traveled ten miles when the sun peeped over the mountains; how cold the air felt as the Turrietas climbed out of the wagon but they were not cold very long: They were all dispersing in different directions, each one trying to find the most heavily loaded piñón tree.

There were many piñón nuts on the ground and these they picked by hand as fast as chickens pick the feed which is strewn for them on the earth. In order to get the nuts which were still in the cones on the trees, Don Teodoro placed a wagon sheet on the ground and as he shook the trees the nuts fell like rain on the sheets. This was easy picking, but it took away the sport which picking it from mother earth affords.

It was a good piñón year and soon every pail was filled. Doña Paula who remained by the wagon, had enough with one tree from which to pick as she had to guard the lunch and care for the piñón nuts which were coming in from each pail.

By noon they had picked a sack full and they were ready to devour any food placed before them. The coffee was already boiling over a camp fire and the lunch which Doña Paula had prepared for her brood was as usual a pleasant surprise.

From a white cloth came a goat's cheese; big round *buñuelos* appeared as she opened a bread basket. In another package which she opened, a roasted leg of kid made everyone's mouth water.

"Where is the chile?" asked José not having seen the big bowl of it by the side of the cheese.

"This is the first red chile this year," said Doña Paula. "It has *espinacito,* sections of the spinal column, in it with plenty of garlic and *orégano,*" the horse mint which they had gathered in the mountains.

The family sat down and soon had eaten every morsel set before them. The cheese was served with the fresh molasses which had come out of the sugar cane press the week before.

The sky began to cloud by mid-afternoon; Don Teodoro whistled for the children as he turned to Doña Paula and said,

"Look at those clouds. We shall have snow before we get home."

It did not take the men long to bring the horses and the family were on their way.

They were a proud outfit with two hundred pounds of piñón nuts to tide them over the winter with visions of pleasant evenings sitting by the fireplace cracking the roasted nuts, and listening to the professional village story teller who would be there to entertain them.

By morning the snow had blanketed the earth and Tilano grumbled when he had to turn out the goats; it meant added work for him. The cows, horses, and goats had to be fed as they could not eat snow and now for sure he knew that he would join the *Aleluyas* where it would be cozy to sit by the warm stove and play the guitar to his heart's content.

HOG KILLING

"Before we know it Christmas will be here," called Doña Paula to Don Teodoro as he put on his gloves to go out to help Tilano. "How is the sow coming?"

"She is ready any day," answered Don Teodoro.

"Well, then, tomorrow we can butcher. The girls will be here to help with the house work."

The day turned out to be a good day for hog killing. The sun was barely showing over the mountains, but Doña Paula already had water boiling in the iron kettle. With her help, the three men of the house had the hog scraped clean in record time and by that time several neighbors had dropped in to help.

The hog was hung down from a limb of the large apricot tree in the yard to cool and drain before they cut it up.

Doña Paula went about making *morcilla,* pork sausage, from the blood which she had taken as the pig had been stuck; while it was still warm she had removed the coagulating substance by working the clots with her hands until they were dissolved and now she had the clear blood. Over the stove she placed a kettle with hog's lard and in it she fried a whole onion cut fine and two cloves of garlic. When it was ready she added the blood and stirred until it separated like scrambled eggs and was well done. To this she added ground coriander seeds, a handful of raisins and shelled piñón nuts; as it cooked she added salt, some sugar and *orégano,* which she pulverized between her hands.

After all the ingredients were added she covered the mixture and left it to cook slowly; part of the mixture she planned to use for the noon meal and the rest she would stuff into the hog casings to be cured for winter eating.

Señá Martina stood by the kitchen table working her fingers through the chile pods, patiently separating the skins from the pulp. The evening before she had prepared the chile pods by removing stems, veins and seeds then placing them in the warm oven to dry out. She always seemed to get more pulp from the soaked chile pods than any one else in the neighborhood and no one ever thought of making the sauce if Señá Martina were around. When she thought the sauce was thick enough, with her hands still thick with chile pulp, she reached for the salt and poured what seemed a handful but it was only a tablespoonful. She washed her hands, then chopped some garlic and between the palms of her hands pulverized some *orégano;* these she carefully added to the chile sauce.

The meat which had been trimmed from the hams and shoulders with fat removed had been cut into strips and these Señá Martina placed in the *adobo,* the chile cure; by morning, it would have soaked enough and would be ready for cooking or to dry for summer use.

The fat was cut into one inch cubes to be made into cracklings, a dainty morsel so much enjoyed by all. The iron kettle with a wood fire under it was ready outdoors to receive the fat for frying, a job which Tilano thoroughly enjoyed and one which was assigned to him. He willingly tended the fire and stirred the lard for he was thinking of the good beans with hog cracklings and of the corn tortillas wrapped around them which Doña Paula put on the table after hog killing. There would also be plenty of lard for *buñuelos* and for *empanaditas,* the fried meat turnovers served at feasts.

There was always a reward for hard labor.

The family and helpers sat down to a supper of *pozole*, lime hominy stew. Señá Martina had been busy the day before making *nixtamal*, the lime hominy, for Doña Paula. In the iron kettle outdoors, she had placed white flint corn to which she had added water and powdered lime and cooked until the skins could be peeled off; then she had taken it out and washed it until all the skins had been removed. Part of the hominy was already drying for winter *pozole;* some would be ground into *harinilla*, the meal for corn *tortillas;* and some would be used fresh now that pork was in season.

CHRISTMAS
FESTIVITIES

4

Long before the sun peeped over the mountains Señá Martina had come in limping to help Doña Paula with the Christmas eve preparations.

"If it were not that I had promised to help you, I would not have stirred from bed today," she said as she folded her shawl and placed it on a bench by the window.

Doña Paula had heard this speech for over thirty years. She knew Señá Martina specialized in aches and pains.

"How are you today?" asked Doña Paula.

"As I was saying, I would not have stirred today, but this is the eve of the birth of our Lord; my rheumatism is getting worse every day. I do not sleep nights and I was awake hours before I saw your light." And in the same breath she asked,

"What do you want me to do?"

"Drink some hot coffee. It will help to warm your joints," answered Doña Paula.

The snow had been falling all morning but it had not kept Doña Paula from cleaning out her adobe oven. Back and forth she went from her kitchen to the patio, wearing a heavy wool dress to keep out the cold. The blue handkerchief tied around her head was bright and gay in the snowy air.

From the back porch she picked up an armful of dry wood. In less than fifteen minutes she had a fire burning in the outdoor oven. When the fire crackled and popped and flames leaped to the top of the oven, she went into the house to make the loaves of bread that would go in as soon as the oven was hot enough.

How beautifully the dough she had made the night before had risen. She almost hated to break it up, particularly the cross she had cut into it. But there was no time for sentiment; in two hours the oven would be ready. She mustn't dawdle on Christmas eve.

Doña Paula took out as much dough as both hands could hold, placing it in another pan while she said to herself, "This will be enough for *molletes,* the sweet rolls."

With a deft hand she kneaded the bread dough and soon was shaping it into beautiful loaves of bread. She patted them softly and laid them side by side in the pans. Then she covered them with a snow-white cloth.

"Leave the *molletes* to me," said Señá Martina. "I like to make sweet rolls."

Señá Martina had no patience with those who used measuring cups and spoons, worrying for fear they would put in an ounce too much of this or that. Her hands were so used to the amounts that without thinking she broke four eggs, beat them thoroughly, and added two handfuls of sugar and a good pinch of anise seed. She reached into the lard pail and took out a handful of fat for her *mollete* dough. She kneaded and kneaded until the dough was carefully mixed; then with a knife she cut a cross in the center of the dough, reciting *Jesús y Cruz,* (Jesus and His Cross) for good luck in her baking.

"How fast time goes," said Doña Paula as Don Teodoro came in the door. "Here it is already nine o'clock; the sun is high and

26

before we know it the day will be gone. Run out and see how the fire goes in the oven." Don Teodoro did not run; he just walked rubbing his hands as he went. "These women," he thought, "make such a fuss over nothing."

As Don Teodoro stirred the coals, he knew the oven was ready. Slowly, easily, he started sweeping out the coals until the floor of the oven shone like a mirror.

There was no need of words; Doña Paula had watched him from the glass on the door and was ready with pan in hand. Like lightning Doña Paula went back and forth to the oven taking pans of bread and *molletes*. When the oven was full, Don Teodoro put the wooden door on.

The snow had stopped falling now, and the sun was shining. The women were putting on their coats and shawls to go and clean the church for Midnight Mass. When Doña Paula and Señá Martina arrived, their friends had donned their aprons and were scrubbing and sweeping. On a corner inside the altar railing, the men were busy with pine boughs, building a crib and manger to hold the Christ Child for the midnight adoration. By twelve o'clock noon all was ready in the church.

After a hurried dinner, while she was drying the dishes, Señá Martina turned to Doña Paula and asked,

"Are we not going to have *bizcochitos* this year, the children enjoy the sugar cookies more than anything else."

"Yes and you are going to make them yourself, as usual. You have a better hand," Doña Paula answered.

She knew Señá Martina wanted to make them and get the praise for somehow she made them more flaky than anyone else.

For *bizcochitos,* the traditional sugar cookies, Señá Martina liked to use native water ground whole wheat flour. She also preferred fresh hog's lard for the shortening; a large handful of lard and two handfuls of sugar went into a bowl. Señá Martina beat and beat with her hands until it was the consistency of whipped cream. Then she added a large pinch of anise seed. In another pan she mixed flour, salt and baking powder (her mistress would have used *tequesquite,* sodium nitrate). "Very little water," thought Señá Martina, "or the *bizcochitos* will be hard." There was no need for cookie cutters; Señá Martina could shape the *bizcochitos* in any form desired and she prided herself on her artistic ability.

There were still the *empanaditas* to make but Doña Paula was not worried. She had cooked the meat that morning, and she had everlasting yeast ready for the dough.

While the *bizcochitos* baked she prepared the filling for the *empanaditas*. A bowl full of meat, cooked dried apples, a large pinch of salt, cinnamon, clove, ground coriander seed, a touch of ginger, two cups of thick molasses and two handfuls of raisins made the filling. This would cook while she made the dough. Señá Martina was there to help with the frying and making of the *empanaditas*.

By five o'clock Doña Paula and Señá Martina had finished, but there were the bread and sweet rolls to take out of the oven. Together they worked removing the bread and *molletes* from the outdoor oven. How good the golden brown bread smelled and how hungry it made them!

As soon as darkness settled in the village, the children with snap sacks started after *aguinaldos*, Christmas gifts. At each door they stopped and sang,

"Oremus, Oremus	"Let us pray, Let us pray
Angelitos somos	Angels from heaven are we
Del Cielo venimos	Asking for gifts in His name
A pedir Aguinaldos y Oremus."	Please do not turn us away."

After the hymn was sung, the door opened and the children received gifts of food. How proud Doña Paula was of her gifts of *molletes, bizcochitos,* and *empanaditas* for the children. She had made enough for them and for the Christmas eve repast.

There was so much to be done before Midnight Mass. The lime hominy had been cooking all day and it was all ready but the seasoning. Doña Paula who was a proud cook had to have everything well seasoned. From a string of chile in her store room she took three pods; she removed stems and seeds and washed the pods. She took the lid off the kettle, added the chile, *orégano,* salt, garlic and onion. Now she could get ready for Mass. The *tamales* which she had made the day before were frozen on the back porch and they could cook while they were at church.

She looked out of her bedroom window. The *hogueras* were already lighted outside the church so she must hurry or she would miss being with her friends by the bonfires.

After the mass, everyone went to the manger to kiss the Infant Jesus' feet. Each one brought a gift for Him — a penny, a nickel, or a dime.

Outside the church everyone was merry, wishing his friends happiness. The one making the wish first, earned a gift from the one to whom it was made. Then they went home to a hot morning breakfast of *pozole, tamales, empanaditas,* and *carne con chile.*

THE WEDDING

5

On the second of January, Doña Refugio sent a letter, composed by the marriage letter writer of the village, to the Turrieta's announcing that she had given her consent to Panchita's marriage to their son, José.

There was much rejoicing in the Turrieta home that day and Tilano was as happy as if he were to be the groom. He had somewhere learned that the groom announced his engagement by firing shots into the air, so before Don Teodoro had realized, Tilano had his gun and the news resounded in the village.

José ran out and was about to strike Tilano when Doña Paula intervened.

"Mother," José said, "we are living in a modern age. What will the neighbors think of us?"

"Never mind the neighbors," answered Doña Paula. "It makes Tilano happy to be a part of this family."

The *prendorio* was held the following Sunday. The bride's home was filled with relatives and friends. The whole village had been invited to the bethrothal feast.

José presented Panchita with a diamond ring. His mother would like to have given her the *memoria,* the intertwined puzzle ring which Don Teodoro had presented her at her bethrothal, but it was old fashioned and her children were of another age and generation.

After the ring ceremony and vows of loyalty and obedience were exchanged, the guests passed on to the dining room for refreshments. There were *bizcochitos,* candy, *empanaditas,* and *marquesotes,* light sponge cakes. There was wine in abundance and no scarcity of hard liquor. In the evening the guests turned to Don Nolasco's hall for the betrothal dance.

On Monday Doña Paula and Don Teodoro called for Panchita; they were taking her to Santa Fe to buy the *donas,* the bride's trousseau. Instead of the truck, on this day, Don Nolasco took his Chevrolet car to celebrate the occasion. He had close dealings with the merchants in the city and with his shrewd reckoning, he could bargain with them and get in on the profit of Don Teodoro's five hundred dollars.

The groom on such an occasion had to show his generosity even if he had to work many a year to pay whatever the bride might spend.

Since the bethrothal feast, José had become a member of Doña Refugio's family and would have to defray all house expenses until after the wedding.

Much thought was given to what day of the week the wedding should be held. "Not on Tuesday," thought Doña Paula. "*'Martes ni te cases ni te embarques,'* 'Tuesday neither wed nor embark,' was a good adage to follow," she said. "On a Monday," she finally decided. January sixteenth would fall on a Monday and there was yet so much to be done in preparation for the wedding.

"Tomorrow we shall go to call on María our Indian *comadre.* She is the best cook we can get for the wedding feast," said Doña Paula to her husband.

At least two days were necessary to prepare all the food. María engaged two helpers and before day break they were baking bread and dried fruit pies in the mud ovens. The fruit was cooked, sweetened and seasoned. Long strips of flaky pastry were placed in bread pans, spread with fruit and covered with more pastry. After these were baked they were cut in squares large enough for generous helpings.

On the wedding eve, María cooked the meat which was to be used in making the *carne con chile* next day and while the meat cooked, she toasted slice after slice of bread for the *capirotada,* the bread pudding which also called for wine. Her helpers grated pounds and pounds of cheese which would go into the making of this favorite dish.

Doña Paula was at hand to advise or help if she were needed.

The morning of the wedding, María and her assistants were up before dawn. Dinner had to be ready by the time the wedding party came back from Santa Fé where the church ceremony took place and Señá Martina came in as usual full of aches and pains but proud that she could still be useful.

"María let me make the bread pudding," she begged.

"Certainly, Señá Martina. Everything is ready but the sugar."

Señá Martina took three cups of sugar and put them in a skillet to brown; she stirred it continuously to keep it from burning and as it turned a golden brown she added enough water to fill the skillet. She then placed layers of toasted bread and cheese and raisins in a pan, sprinkled cinnamon over this mixture, and added the syrup which was just enough to cover it. With a heaping tablespoon of lard, the bread pudding went into the oven to thicken; the wine would be added later.

María cut the cooked beef into small pieces while the onion and garlic browned in the fat; she then added the meat and mixed it well. In a bowl she dissolved some chile powder and put it with the meat and enough of the stock to make a good thick sauce. In the back of the stove it would cook slowly and not dry out.

The rice had been cooked in the milk. The raisins and eggs would be put in last. Señá Martina who always claimed to have a good hand for making egg whites stand in peaks was beating the eggs. She turned to María and said,

"It is not everyone who can beat eggs. It is all in one's hands. I know persons who cannot even create a foam in eggs."

"How many raisins shall I put in?" asked María to please Señá Martina.

"Two handfuls," she answered.

After the raisins went in, the egg whites which had now been mixed with the beaten yolks went into the rice. A short boil and it was ready for the flavoring. Carefully, Señá Martina sprinkled cinnamon over it and placed it by the window to cool.

A long table had been placed in the center of the living room which had been cleared of all furniture except benches and chairs. The table cloth used for special occasions covered the table. Here were placed the refreshments: *Bizcochitos,* cakes, candies, pies, wine and whiskey. Only the men took whiskey.

José and Panchita alighted from the car as it reached the patio, then formed the procession to the wedding march which the musicians hired for the day were playing. After hand shakes and good wishes, everyone was invited to the table to drink to the health and happiness of the newly married couple.

In the dining room everything was ready. The table was set with Doña Refugio's best linen, silver and china. There were bowls of *pozole, carne con chile,* macaroni with tomatoes, mashed potatoes and roasted mutton in platters. Fried bread and the bread baked in the mud oven the day before were piled a foot high in pans. The dessert was on the table too. *Capirotada,* rice pudding, pies and canned fruit were served in deep bowls. The guests had their choice but everyone felt obligated, as a sign of courtesy, to taste some of each.

At four o'clock the guests were still being served but the wedding party had moved on to Don Nolasco's hall for the dance. A canopy from bed sheets and decorated with paper flowers was constructed at the back of the hall. A large mirror surrounded by letters spelling José and Panchita finished the decorations. Doña Refugio's best chairs were placed inside the canopy for the bride and groom.

The music was furnished by the village musicians, a fiddler and a guitar player. The grand march was led by José and Panchita and everyone joined in — young and old. Old time dances were much in evidence and the *vals chiquillado* furnished everyone with much mirth; in this waltz the partners exchanged verses. The lady sat on a chair and her partner favored her with a verse to which she had to reply; some of the verses were complimentary and others humorous. There were quadrilles, schottisches, *varsoviana* and other native dances enjoyed by all.

After the dance came the *entrega* when the *padrinos,* the best man and bride's maid, turn the newlyweds over to their parents for their blessing by reciting appropriate verses.

El padrino y la madrina	The best man and bride's maid
Ya saben su obligación	well know their obligation
De entregar a los desposados	To turn over the newlyweds
Y échenles su bendición	to the parents
	Who will give them their
	parental blessing

The guests had accompanied the wedding party to the bride's home for the *entrega* and the wedding was over.

LENT

6

A week passed and life went on as before. Doña Paula and Señá Martina were washing wheat for sprouting. Lent was not far off and they had to have *panocha,* sprouted wheat pudding, for the meatless days.

The wheat was put in sacks after it was thoroughly washed and was then placed behind the kitchen stove where it would be kept warm.

In two days the sprouts began to show and it was ready to dry.

In cold and damp weather, it took two weeks for the wheat to dry; it was then taken to the grist mill to be ground into flour. Don Teodoro was proud to bring back six *almudes* (about 4½ bushels). They could sell flour and still have enough to supply their table.

"Lent is early this year," said Doña Paula to Señá Martina. "In another week Ash Wednesday will be here and we might as well start making *panocha.*"

"Just as well," answered Señá Martina who could hardly wait to eat the delicacy. It was a food she could enjoy without aid of chewing apparatus.

Tilano came in with the large copper kettle which was always used for the occasion. Señá Martina had measured in handfuls, two parts of sprouted wheat meal and one part of whole wheat flour. Slowly she added boiling water to the mixture stirring it with the *meneador,* the wooden stirring stick, until it was well mixed then she set it aside to steam for a while. In the meantime she caramelized some sugar and when it was ready she added it to the other ingredients.

"Are you going to add sugar?" asked Doña Paula as she watched Señá Martina mixing it with the stirring stick.

"Yes, the older I get, the more I crave sweet things and the children like it sweet too," she answered.

Doña Paula went outside to start the mud oven while Señá Martina cooked the sprouted wheat pudding on the kitchen stove, which in an hour of quick cooking would be ready for the oven outdoors where it would cook all night at slow heat and next day come out a dark brown, lustrous and thick. The oven door had to be sealed tight with mud, so no steam could escape. Even the oven's smoke stack had to be closed tightly.

On Ash Wednesday, Doña Paula soaked some of the dried squash. With a dash of chile powder and some cheese this would make a delicious dish. She had dried peas cooking since early morning and peas must be flavored with a pinch of *chimajá,* wild parsley, to give it the right flavor. Dried green chile was also soaking. She had not decided whether to make *torrejas,* egg fritters, with it or plain seasoned chile. Señá Martina would probably drop in and she liked to put her fingers in it. Doña Paula still had to make the dough for the whole wheat *tortillas,* anyway.

Limping as usual, before Doña Paula had had time to wish for her, Señá Martina was there. She removed her shawl and folded it carefully as was her custom.

From the warming oven, Señá Martina took a skillet; she placed some fat in it, in which she fried onions and garlic. With her hands she worked the soaked chile, then added it to the onion and garlic.

"I shall make the *tortillas* while you prepare the peas," she said to Doña Paula. She formed the dough into balls and each ball she spread out into a round cake. She tested the top of the stove with her hand and when it was ready she started cooking each *tortilla* until it was dotted with brown specks on both sides. How lovely and round the *tortillas* looked as she stood them on end so they would not get soggy.

The family came in one by one to sit to a Lenten meal. The surprise was *panocha* for the dessert.

Señá Martina had visions of a good Lent. She had helped Doña Paula prepare lambs quarters, purslane, steamed corn, dried fruits and other foods without which the fast days would have been uninteresting. She knew one by one would appear on the table on Wednesdays and Fridays of Lent, not to think as far as Holy Week.

THE WAKE

7

Lent seemed hardly past, when spring came to El Alamo. Somehow Señá Martina seemed feebler than usual. "It was not the usual malady of aches and pains," thought Doña Paula. For several days she had not complained and it was not natural.

In the evening, Don Teodoro said to his wife. "The kids are getting big enough to butcher. We shall bring one in tomorrow."

Doña Paula thought of Señá Martina. She always made *morcilla,* the blood pudding, for her.

After the dishes were finished, she stepped over to her friend's house and found that Señá Martina was really failing. Doña Paula tried to cheer her by making her feel necessary to the next day's chore, but Señá Martina said,

"I cannot help you tomorrow; you can get along without me. Do not forget to chop up all the cleaned intestines. Catch the blood and remove the coagulating substance by working it with your fingers until all the clots are removed before it gets cold; then fry onion and garlic, put the blood and intestines in it and flavor with *oregano.* After you clean the stomach, stuff it with the blood mixture and cook it. When it is done bring me a small portion. Cook the spinal column with red chile and season it right."

Next morning at day break Tilano and Don Teodoro with Doña Paula's help were at their task of kid butchering.

Don Teodoro tied the right front leg of the kid to its right hind leg then tied its left hind leg to a beam in the ceiling of the store room. Doña Paula with a pail in hand was ready to receive the blood as Don Teodoro slit the animal's throat. While it was still hot she removed the coagulating substance as Señá Martina had instructed her. She then put on her bandana and walked over to see how Señá Martina was feeling.

Señá Martina did not recognize her friend and Doña Paula knew that she was nearing the end of her journey, so she hurriedly sent word to Don Nolasco to call for the priest while she prepared the house and the patient for the last sacraments.

Peacefully Señá Martina breathed her last and as her tears flowed freely, Doña Paula thought, "She died as she lived, contented, helping others to the end and causing no one any inconvenience with a lingering illness."

Señá Martina's children were there but Doña Paula took over, wishing she had done more for her while she lived.

She was glad that they had butchered a kid as there would be fresh meat for the chile. In the *despensa,* the store room, she still had some of the pork which Señá Martina had cured and dried and this would go into the *pozole* which Señá Martina had also made.

Doña Paula could not hold the tears back as she said to Don Teodoro,

"How well our departed friend prepared everything for her own wake."

The men were out in the graveyard digging the grave and friends were dropping in to see Señá Martina, as she lay on the improvised bier which Doña Paula had prepared on a table with her finest sheets for Señá Martina's last bed. Lighted candles surrounded the bier.

By supper time the house was filled with friends and neighbors. The men were out in the patio discussing politics, the weather and current events but the women dressed in black and the older ones with shawls over their heads sat in every room of the house quietly thinking about death and life.

The rosary was said by the village *rezador,* the official one who prays, and after it was finished the men were called to partake of the evening meal which was as much a part of the wake as the prayers and the corpse. By midnight the men had all been fed; then the women took their turn.

The food served at the wake was similar to one served at a wedding feast. There was *carne con chile, pozole, buñuelos,* rice pudding and *capirotada.*

Next morning the priest arrived by eight o'clock to say the Mass for the departed one. The men carried the body on a litter as there was no coffin for Señá Martina; she had asked to be given an Indian burial. She had often said to Doña Paula, "I do not want a coffin. There is no need for pomp and expense because once we are dead nothing matters anymore. The coffin rots and we return to the earth as was intended."

After the funeral the participants returned to the house of the *dolientes,* Señá Martina's mourners. Everyone had already expressed their sympathy but it was the custom to accompany the family to their home and again offer their condolence and help.

Doña Paula was the chief mourner for Señá Martina, who had been closer to her than even her own mother. She had depended on her since she came to El Alamo as a bride and theirs had been a silent friendship, deeper than words could express and only the heart could feel.

THE COOKBOOK

8

The recipes which follow are New Mexican in character; an amalgamation of the different influences which have been evident in the state since and before the Spanish conquest.

When we think of New Mexican foods, naturally the chile dishes come first. New Mexico is well adapted to chile culture and therefore we have become accustomed to the pungent flavor which it gives to our foods. We like it and we have developed ways of preparing chile dishes so as to give them the delightful taste which makes them so popular.

In order to have the dishes taste as one has eaten them in the New Mexican homes or genuine New Mexican restaurants, one must use New Mexican products. These can be obtained commercially, of course, but if substitutions are necessary, be prepared for a difference in flavor. Mexican chile peppers do not have the same taste as New Mexican peppers but many people enjoy their savor and may even enjoy the change. Quite often the commercial chile powder has been flavored so it is well to taste it before adding any of the seasonings.

Chicos, the dried green steamed corn, can be made successfully by steaming corn with part of the husks in a kettle over the cook stove and then drying it outdoors.

Powdered chile which can be bought in the stores can be substituted for the chile pulp obtained from the chile pods; canned green chile may be used in the dishes which require the freshly prepared product; cow's milk makes a good cheese and good substitutes for goat's cheese are the strong imported cheeses. Lime hominy is easily made — remember to always use an enameled or iron kettle for its preparation — never an aluminum one.

The herbs for flavoring can be purchased almost anywhere in the United States. Those of you who have facilities for gardens may find it fun to grow them.

Unless otherwise noted, recipes serve the average New Mexican household, six persons. As to the breads, they are ample, or more, for a day's eating.

Please do not shudder at the thought of eating blood — it is a delightful dish which has no identity with the raw product. This is the way the native New Mexicans prepare it:

When an animal is butchered the blood is caught as the neck of the victim is slit. While the blood is still warm quickly one works it with one's fingers removing a substance which appears like strings in the blood. When no more strings or clots appear and the blood is clear it is ready for preparation. See *Morcilla* page 55.

Table of Abbreviations

t. — teaspoon	lb. — pound
T. — tablespoon	pt. — pint
c. — cup	qt. — quart

Use level measurements except where specified.

CHILE

Salsa de Chile
Chile Sauce (with chile powder)

1 qt. boiling water	8 T. chile powder
3 T. fat	1 clove chopped garlic
1 t. salt	

Add fat and salt to boiling water. Make a paste of the chile powder with cold water and add to the salted boiling water. Stir until well blended and cook to the consistency of tomato sauce. Add chopped garlic. For a thicker sauce, add more chile powder.

Salsa de Chile
Chile Sauce (from chile pods)

24 dried chile pods	1 clove chopped garlic
1 qt. boiling water	1 t. salt
1 T. fat	1 t. *orégano*

Method i

Wash chile pods; remove stems, seeds and veins. Place pods in a warm oven for 10 minutes, watching them carefully that they do not scorch. Take out pods; add boiling water and let soak until peppers are soft. With hands work chile pods until pulp is separated from skins. Remove skins.

Place fat in skillet, fry chopped garlic; add chile pulp and seasonings. Cook for 5 minutes.

Method ii

Proceed to prepare chile pods as for Method I. Instead of placing pods in the oven pour boiling water over them and cook until tender. Cool, remove from water and pass through food mill or colander. Occasionally add some of the water in which it was cooked to thin it down as the pulp passes through the colander. Prepare the pulp as in Method I.

Salsa de Chile con Tomates
Chile Sauce with Tomatoes

2 T. fat
1 clove chopped garlic
2 T. chopped onion
2 c. tomatoes (canned or fresh)

2 c. chile sauce or 4. T. chile powder
1 t. salt
1 t. *orégano*

Fry garlic and onion in fat. Add tomatoes and cook until thick; add chile sauce and let it boil for 5 minutes. If chile powder is used, make a paste with a little cold water and add to the tomatoes. Season.

Chile Verde
Green Chile

12 green chile peppers
1 clove garlic

1 t. finely chopped onion
1 t. salt

Wash chile pods; snip ends. Place in oven or broiler and roast until skins blister. Place in a pan and cover with damp cloth; let steam for a few minutes. Remove skins by starting at the stem end and working down. Take off stems and squeeze out seeds. Chop; rub bowl with garlic and place chopped chile in it. Add onion and salt. Serve.

CORN DISHES

For the preparation of corn dishes, any of the edible varieties of corn may be used. In New Mexico we have two varieties commonly used: These are the *concho* and the flint. For corn *tortillas,* to be used for *enchiladas,* we prefer the blue Indian corn but any of the white varieties may be substituted. The *tortillas* already prepared can be purchased in cans or in packages. The packaged *tortillas* should be kept under refrigeration, if not used immediately, as otherwise they have a tendency to turn sour.

Nixtamal
Lime Hominy

2 heaping T. slaked   1 qt. dried whole kernels
powdered lime   of corn
2 qts. water

Mix lime with water and stir until well blended. Add to corn which has been placed in an iron or enameled kettle. Cook until hulls loosen from the kernels. Drain and wash thoroughly, removing the skins by rubbing corn between the hands. It may require two or three baths to remove the lime when the corn is to be used for *tamales*. For *tortillas,* less washing is required; one rinse is sufficient.

Tortillas de Nixtamal
Lime Hominy Tortillas

The corn *tortillas* have a variety of uses in the New Mexican menus: They may be used for making *enchiladas;* for *tacos;* for *tostadas;* or to eat as bread with New Mexican foods.

The prepared *nixtamal* (p. 49) is ground into meal which is called *masa.* A food chopper does a good job if passed through the coarse knife and then through the fine one. After grinding it, if the *masa* is too dry, add enough water to keep it of a good consistency — not too moist nor too dry — just enough to hold together.

Shape the *masa* into round balls of desired size. Place a damp towel on a bread board; put ball of *masa* on this and fold other end of towel over it. With a small board pat the *masa* until it has been pressed down into a *tortilla* about ⅛ inch in thickness. It may be necessary to pat it down with the hand to get it properly shaped. To do this: Uncover the *masa,* wet the hand and pat the dough into a round shape and the desired thickness. (The New Mexican housewife does not use a board; she shapes the *tortillas* between her hands but it takes skill.) Cook *tortillas* on both sides on a greased griddle.

The prepared meal, called *harillina* may be purchased for the making of *tortillas;* when this is used proceed as follows: To 2 cups of *harillina,* add enough boiling water to acquire a medium hard dough — a dough that holds together without splitting. Proceed to make *tortillas* as those made from the *nixtamal.*

49

ENCHILADAS

Fry the *tortillas* in hot deep fat. If you like a rolled *enchilada,* place grated cheese, chopped onion, and chile sauce in the center of the *tortilla,* roll, place on plate and cover with more chile sauce.

The New Mexican way of making *enchiladas* is as follows: Dip the *tortilla* in the chile sauce, place on a plate, add grated cheese and chopped onion, cover with another *tortilla;* sprinkle with cheese and onion; then pour plenty of chile sauce over it.

In making *enchiladas* for a large dinner this method may be followed: Dip *tortilla* in chile sauce; sprinkle with cheese and onion and add chile sauce; place another *tortilla* on top and proceed as before until four to six *tortillas* have been placed on top of each other. Cut into four or six servings depending on size desired. When served on plate pour more chile sauce over it.

A fried egg is often served as a garnish on the *enchiladas.*

TAMALES

The ground nixtamal may be used for making *tamales.* The *masa* for these should be of a fine texture. There are preparations in the market of different trade names which can be used for making *tamales.* If these are not available, white corn meal may be used as follows: To 2 cups corn meal add ⅛ t. powdered slaked lime; add enough water to make a medium dough.

After the *masa* is prepared beat enough lard or other fat into it until it is of a slick consistency. Add salt to taste (it requires considerable salt). Prepare corn husks by trimming the ends. Wash and place to soak in warm water.

Prepare *carne con chile* (p. 53) making it quite thick so it does not run.

Spread each corn husk with *masa* about ¼ inch thick; in the center place 2 t. *carne con chile.* Fold sides of corn husks together, then top and bottom. Tie with strips of corn husks. (If husks are large enough it is not necessary to tie them.)

Steam for 25 minutes or cook in pressure cooker for 10 minutes at 15 pounds pressure.

50

Pozole de Nixtamal
Lime Hominy Stew

2 c. lime hominy (p. 49)	1 medium onion
6 c. water	4 dried red chile pods
1 lb. pork ribs or other	2 t. salt
pork cuts suitable	2 cloves chopped garlic
for boiling	2 t. *orégano*
½ lb. pork rind	2 t. saffron

Cook hominy until corn kernels begin to burst; add meat, pork rind, onion, chile pods (seeds and stems removed). When meat is nearly done add seasonings. Cook well done. If the pressure cooker is used, cook corn without pressure until kernels begin to burst; then add meat, pork rind and chile pods. Close cooker and cook 30 minutes at 15 pounds pressure. Open, add seasonings and cook slowly for at least 15 minutes.

Pozole de Chicos
Dried Steamed Corn Stew

Dried green corn which has been steamed before drying is known as *chicos*. This product has a delightful flavor.

Chicos can be substituted for the lime hominy in the recipe given above. *Chicos* do not burst in cooking, they swell as other dried green corn.

Chicos Quebrados
Cracked Chicos

Cracked *chicos* are a common Lenten dish.

2 T. fat	1 c. *chicos*
½ small onion	1 c. chile sauce or 4 T.
1 clove chopped garlic	powdered chile
	1 t. salt

Crack the corn in the food chopper. Cook until tender in enough water to cover. Fry onion and garlic in fat; add drained *chicos*, chile sauce or chile powder and salt. Add enough of the liquid in which the *chicos* were cooked so that they do not have too dry a consistency. Cook enough to blend with the chile flavor.

51

CARNES
Meats

Roasts, steaks and chops are not a common fare on the native New Mexican's tables. Meat must be properly seasoned with herbs or vegetables to make it palatable and interesting.

Kid meat in summer is an exquisite dish to our New Mexican palates. Mutton may be a substitute but it lacks the delicate flavor of *cabrito*.

ALBÓNDIGAS
Meat Balls

1½ lbs. round steak or other cuts suitable for grinding	2 cloves chopped garlic
6 T. blue cornmeal or 1 c. bread crumbs	2 t. ground coriander seed
2 eggs, beaten	1 t. pepper
2 t. salt	½ onion chopped fine

Grind meat; add other ingredients and mix well. Form into balls the size of a robin's egg.

SOUP

4 T. fat	2 t. dried mint leaves
2 T. flour	1 t. saffron
4 c. water	Salt

Melt fat and brown flour in it. Add water and seasonings. As it boils, drop meat balls into it and cook until meat is well done.

The meat balls may be cooked in a chile sauce with tomatoes (p. 48) instead of the soup.

CARNE ADOBADA
Cured Pork

Any tender cut of pork may be used for curing. Remove fat from pork; cut meat into strips about 3 inches long and 2 inches thick. Place in chile sauce made from chile pods (p. 47). Leave in chile cure for at least 24 hours or until ready to be used. (Season chile with garlic and *orégano* but do not cook.)

Keep in refrigerator until used.

To Prepare

Take out as much of the meat as needed for preparation. Cut in small pieces; fry in hot lard until done. Add some of the chile sauce in which it was cured and more if necessary to keep it from drying. Cover and cook slowly until well done.

Carne Asada de Res
Beef Roast

3 lbs. loin roast	½ c. orange juice
1 c. tomatoes	1 t. *orégano*
1 large onion sliced	2 T. vinegar
2 red peppers	Salt

Cut roast into thick strips. Place in roaster. Add tomatoes, onion, peppers (stems and seeds removed), orange juice and other ingredients. Cook in a moderate oven until well done. If it dries while cooking, add hot water as needed.

Carne con Chile Colorado
Meat with Red Chile

It is not advisable to use hamburger for this dish. The genuine dish must never have a greasy film. Round steak cut in cubes and browned in fat is suitable for making *carne con chile* but boiling meat gives it the flavor that the New Mexicans prefer.

1½ lbs. boiling meat (beef or pork)	1 t. salt
2 T. fat	1 t. *orégano* (if desired)
2 T. flour	1 clove chopped garlic
2 c. chile sauce or 8 T. chile powder	1 c. meat stock or tomatoes

Cook meat until tender but not too well done. Cut into small cubes. Fry in fat and add flour. Remove from fire. Add chile powder or chile sauce. Season. Add meat stock or tomatoes. If chile powder is used, increase stock or tomatoes by 1 cup. Cook for ½ hour or until meat is tender.

CARNE CON CHILE VERDE
Meat with Green Chile

1½ lbs. boiling meat	1 clove chopped garlic
2 T. fat	2 c. meat stock or tomatoes
1 c. canned green chile	Salt
or freshly prepared	

Cook meat until tender but not well done. Cut into small cubes. Fry in fat; add green chile, garlic and liquid. Add salt and cook until meat is done.

CHILES RELLENOS
Stuffed Green Peppers
Filling

1 lb. boiling meat	2 t. ground coriander seed
4 c. water	2 T. chopped onion
1 c. raisins	2 cloves chopped garlic
1 t. salt	12 green chiles
½ t. ground clove	

Cook meat. Grind; add raisins and seasonings. Mix well. Prepare green chile by roasting and peeling as discussed on p. 48. Leave stems on peppers; slit in center and remove seeds; stuff with filling and dip into a batter made as follows:

Separate 6 eggs; beat whites until stiff and fold lightly beaten yolks. Add 6 T. flour or 4 T. bran and salt to taste. Dip stuffed peppers into this batter and fry in deep fat or oil until well browned on all sides. Serve with the following tomato sauce:

4 T. fat	1 c. meat stock
2 T. flour	1 c. strained tomatoes or
	tomato sauce

Brown flour in fat; add meat stock and tomatoes. Drop fried stuffed peppers into this sauce and let them stand in it for a few minutes before serving.

Espinacito de Cabrito con Chile
Kids Spinal Column (or Back Bone) with Chile

The sections of the spinal
  column
Enough water to cook
Salt to taste

1 clove garlic
1 t. *orégano*
2 c. chile sauce

Cook spinal column until well done. Separate sections. When cooked add the other ingredients and cook until thick. If there is too much liquid before adding chile sauce, take some out so that the sauce will be of a medium consistency.

Morcilla de Cabrito
Kid Blood Pudding

1 qt. kid's blood
2 c. kid's tripe (third
  stomach) cut in pieces
2 c. small intestines
  cut in pieces
4 T. fat

1 medium chopped onion
2 cloves chopped garlic

1 t. *orégano*
1 t. dried mint
2 t. salt

If the tripe is used, wash thoroughly; pour boiling water over it, scrape scum. To clean the intestines pour water through opening and wash clean.

Fry onion and garlic in fat; add blood which has been prepared (p. 46). Stir until it separates similar to scrambled eggs. Add tripe and intestines. Season. If it seems too dry add a little water and cook until tripe is tender. It should have the consistency of scrambled eggs.

Morcilla de Cerdo
Pork Blood Sausage

1 qt. hog's blood
4 T. fat
1 small chopped onion
1 clove chopped garlic
1 c. raisins

½ c. piñón nuts, shelled
1 t. *orégano*
1 t. coriander seed
1 T. sugar
2 t. salt

Prepare blood (p. 46). Fry blood in fat until it has the consistency of scrambled eggs. Add onion, garlic, raisins, piñón nuts and seasonings. Add enough water to keep moist while it cooks. Cover and simmer for 30 minutes.

Pierna de Carnero
Leg of Lamb

1 leg of lamb	3 T. fat
3 cloves garlic	2 T. vinegar in which mint leaves have stood for 24 hours
	Salt and pepper

Stick cloves of garlic in leg of lamb. Rub with fat; add vinegar, salt and pepper. Roast in a moderate oven until well done.

AVES DE CORRAL
Poultry

As with meat, the New Mexican cook rarely serves poultry without the addition of a sauce or a vegetable.

Arroz con Pollo
Rice with Chicken

1 cooking hen, cut in pieces	1 t. saffron
1 c. rice	1 t. mint
½ c. olive oil or other fat	Salt
1 large chopped onion	Pepper

Cook chicken in plenty of water until done. Remove from stock. Strain soup and in it cook the rice until fluffy and tender. Melt fat, fry onion; add rice and seasonings. Keep rice moist but not watery. The chicken may be put in the rice and served with it or each may be served separately.

GALLINA RELLENA
Stuffed Fowl

1 roasting fowl	1 t. coriander seed
(12 to 15 lbs.)	
¼ lb. butter	1 t. cinnamon
1 lb. cooked beef	½ t. cloves
2 c. raisins	1 c. meat stock
1 c. shelled piñón nuts	½ c. red wine
2 squares melted	Salt
chocolate	

Clean and prepare fowl for roasting as usual. Rub inside with butter. Grind beef, add raisins and other ingredients except wine. Cook until thick. Add wine and let come to a boil. Stuff fowl as with other stuffing and roast until tender.

PESCADO
Fish

New Mexico being an inland state does not have the variety of fish that other states enjoy. The most common fish is the mountain trout which draws fishermen from all parts of the country. Dried shrimp has been used as a Lenten food since early colonial days. This came from Mexico and it is yet very commonly used.

TORREJAS DE CAMARÓN
Shrimp Fritters

3 eggs	2 t. salt
1 c. canned or ½ c.	½ t. baking powder
dry powdered shrimp	Fat
4 T. flour	3 c. chile sauce

Separate eggs; beat whites until stiff. Add yolks slightly beaten, shrimp, flour, baking powder and salt. Drop by tablespoonsful in hot fat. Brown well on both sides. Drop into hot chile sauce (p. 47). Serve.

TRUCHA FRITA
Fried Trout

1 large or several small trout	1 T. vinegar
½ c. oil or fat	1 t. parsley
1 small chopped onion	1 T. butter
1 clove chopped garlic	½ lemon sliced

Clean trout; fry. Add onion and cook until done. Add vinegar to parsley, garlic and melted butter. Pour over fish and onions. Garnish with parsley and lemon slices.

QUESO
Cheese

One rarely drops into a New Mexican rural home of a morning that one does not see a pan or pail of milk on the back of the stove in preparation for making cheese. It may be goat's or cow's milk, but cheese is a very important dish in the diet. It is eaten as dessert with cane molasses or sorghum and more modernly with jelly or jam.

QUESO FRESCO
Native Fresh Cheese

1 gal. sweet milk	4 junket tablets or 1/10 rennet tablet

Warm milk to 90° F. temperature. Dissolve junket or rennet tablet in 4 t. water; stir into the milk and blend thoroughly. Let stand in warm place for ½ hour. When set, cut into small pieces with knife or hand. Remove as much whey as possible. Pour curd into cloth bag and let drain until all whey has disappeared.

58

CHILE VERDE CON QUESO
Green Chile with Cheese

3 T. fat	1 c. canned green chile
3 T. chopped onion	1 t. salt
1 clove chopped garlic	1 c. thinly sliced cheese

Melt fat; fry onion and garlic. Add chopped green chile and salt. Add cheese and cook on top of stove until cheese melts.

CHONGOS
Cheese Twists

1 fresh cheese	1 stick cinnamon or ½ t.
(from 1 gal. milk)	powdered cinnamon
2 c. sugar	2 c. water

Use curd which has not been thoroughly drained. Make a syrup from the sugar and water, flavoring it with the cinnamon. (If powdered cinnamon is used, mix with sugar before adding to water.) Drop slightly drained curd into syrup by spoonfuls. Cook slowly until firm but not tough. Remove cheese from syrup and boil syrup until thick. Serve over cheese and sprinkle with cinnamon.

QUESADILLAS
Cheese Turnovers
Filling

½ native fresh cheese	1 t. cinnamon
2 eggs	1 t. salt
½ c. sugar	Milk

Cut cheese finely; add beaten eggs, sugar mixed with cinnamon, salt and enough milk to make a medium paste.

MASA
Dough

1½ c. flour	8 T. shortening
1 t. baking powder	4 to 6 T. water
1 t. salt	

Sift flour with baking powder and salt; blend in shortening and add water. Roll out dough ⅛ inch thick. Cut in rounds about 3 inches in diameter. Place 1 tablespoon of cheese filling in each round; fold over and turn edges. Bake in hot oven until well browned.

HUEVOS
Eggs

TORREJAS
Egg Fritters

3 eggs	1 t. salt
2 T. bran	6 T. fat

Separate eggs; beat whites until stiff. Add yolks lightly beaten. Fold in bran and add salt. Drop into hot fat by spoonfuls. Brown on both sides.

TORREJAS CON CHILE
Chile Fritters

Heat two cups prepared chile sauce (p. 47). Drop egg fritters into the sauce and let come to a boil. Set back from fire but keep hot until served.

TORTILLA ESPANOLA
Spanish Omelet

4 medium potatoes	1 t. pepper
6 T. fat	6 eggs
1 t. salt	

Cut potatoes into small cubes; fry in fat until brown. Add salt and pepper. Beat eggs well and pour them over the cooked potatoes, stir well until the eggs begin to curdle. Cook over slow fire. Turn and cook on the under side being careful not to overcook.

VEGETALES
Vegetables

CALABACITAS CON CHILE VERDE
Summer Squash and Green Chile

4 T. fat	Salt and pepper
½ small chopped onion	½ c. grated native or
4 medium-sized summer	American cheese
squash	¼ c. milk
½ c. chopped green chile	

Melt fat; add onion and diced squash. Cook until medium done. Add milk, green chile and seasonings; cover and cook 15 minutes. Remove from fire and add grated cheese. In place of green chile, 1 c. canned whole kernel corn may be added.

COCIDO DE GARBANZO
Chick Pea Stew

1 c. garbanzo	1 c. chopped ham
6 c. water	1 c. Spanish or Mexican
1 small onion sliced	sausage
1 clove chopped garlic	1 t. *orégano*
	Salt and pepper

Soak chick pea overnight. Drain and add boiling water. Cook and when partly done add onion, garlic, ham and sausage. Cook until chick peas are tender. Season with *orégano,* salt and pepper. A chile pepper added before it is quite done gives it a special flavor.

ALVERJONES MADUROS
Dried Mature Peas

1 c. dried peas	2 T. fat
5 c. water	1 t. *orégano*
1 sliced onion	1 t. ground coriander seed
1 clove chopped garlic	Salt to taste

Soak peas overnight. Drain and add boiling water. When they have cooked 1 hour, skim off skins which come to the top; add onion and garlic; cook until tender and the water has boiled down. Mash; add fat, *orégano,* coriander seed and salt. Cook a few minutes to bring out seasoning.

61

FRIJOLES
Beans

The *pinto,* a spotted bean, and the *bolita,* a round light brown bean, are the varieties widely used in New Mexico. Other of the brown varieties may be used, but they do not have quite the flavor which is characteristic of the native species.

In order to obtain the right flavor, beans must be cooked for a long time at a low temperature. If the pressure cooker is used, beans must be cooked uncovered for at least 20 minutes after the pressure has been released.

RECIPE

1 c. beans	1 t. sugar
5 c. water	4 T. fat or ½ c. diced
1 clove garlic	salt pork
	Salt to taste

Wash and soak beans for at least 12 hours. Cook in boiling water, adding the garlic and sugar when they are put on to cook. If beans dry while cooking add boiling water each time. It takes from 3 to 6 hours to cook beans, depending on altitude and softness of the water. (If salt pork is used add after beans have cooked at least ½ hour.) If salt pork is not used proceed as follows: Melt fat, add 2 T. flour and brown. Add beans and cook a few minutes to bring out the flavor.

FRIJOLES MACHACADOS
Mashed Beans

Using the above recipe, when beans are thoroughly cooked and the liquid reduced so that it barely covers them, mash them slightly with a potato masher. Melt 4 T. fat; brown 2 T. flour in it and add to beans. Salt and let cook for 5 or 10 minutes.

Frijoles Refritos
Refried Beans

Left over beans lose their flavor unless fat is added when reheated. If left over beans have not been mashed, mash them; melt enough fat (1 T. for every cup) and fry beans in it. A little grated cheese added will give them a special flavor.

Papas y Chile
Potatoes and Chile

4 T. fat	1 c. canned green or freshly prepared chile
2 small onions chopped fine	4 good sized potatoes cooked and diced

Fry onion in fat; add potatoes and cook until fat has been absorbed. Add chile and salt; cover and cook for 15 minutes. Red chile sauce or chile powder may be used in place of the green chile. If the powder is used, add enough water to obtain a thick consistency.

Pan de Papas
Potato Loaf

4 eggs	1 clove chopped garlic
2 t. salt	2 T. minced bacon
1 t. pepper	4 c. cooked diced potatoes
½ c. milk	2 T. olive oil

Beat egg whites until stiff; add slightly beaten yolks, salt, pepper, milk and potatoes. Fry onion and garlic with bacon and mix with other ingredients. Melt olive oil in casserole and put potato mixture in it. Bake until egg sets.

63

ARROZ
Rice

ARROZ A LA ESPANOLA
Spanish Rice

1 c. rice	2 T. sweet peppers or
4 T. diced salt pork	2 hot green peppers
1 small chopped onion	4 c. tomatoes
1 clove garlic	Salt

Wash and clean rice. Dry thoroughly. Fry salt pork, onion, sweet pepper and garlic; when browned remove from fat: Add rice to fat and fry until brown. Add tomatoes and cook until rice is fluffy and well done. If the rice dries during the cooking period add a little water. (If canned green chile is used add to rice after it has browned.) The fried onion, salt pork and green pepper may be put back in the rice before adding tomatoes.

SOPA DE ARROZ
Dry Rice Soup

4 T. fat	2 c. cooked salted rice
½ small chopped onion	2 t. saffron
1 clove garlic	1 t. dry mint leaves
	2 hard cooked eggs

Fry onion and garlic in fat; add rice and season with saffron and mint. Cook until seasoning is well blended with rice. Garnish with hard cooked eggs. Serve. (This may be used as a first course in a dinner or in place of potatoes at any meal.)

VERDURAS
Greens

There are many wild plants used as greens by the New Mexican cook. The most common are lambs' quarters and purslane. The Indians prefer *waco,* the bee weed, and the leaves of wild parsley. Spinach, beet or turnip greens may be substituted for *quelites.* There is no substitute for purslane. Purslane is a prolific weed growing in gardens and fields.

QUELITES
Lambs' Quarters

2 T. fat	1 T. chile seed
2 T. chopped onion	1 t. salt
2 c. finely chopped, cooked greens	½ c. cooked whole beans

Fry onion in fat; add greens and season with chile seeds, salt and beans.

VERDOLAGAS
Purslane

3 c. purslane	1 c. cooked shredded meat (jerkey preferred)
4 T. fat or ½ c. diced salt pork	1 t. ground coriander seed
2 T. chopped onion	Salt to taste

Wash purslane leaving stems. Fry onion in fat; add purslane and cook until tender. Add meat, coriander and salt. Cover and cook for 5 minutes. (A substitute for jerky in this dish may be prepared by placing ground meat in the oven and drying it until crisp.)

65

ENSALADAS

Salads

While salads are not typically New Mexican, yet no menu today is complete without them. The recipes given for salads are those which because of their flavor or texture blend with New Mexican foods.

Ensalada de Aguacate
Avocado Salad

1 clove garlic	1 small onion
1 large firm avocado	1 small head of lettuce
2 fresh tomatoes	Salt
4 medium sized radishes	4 T. olive oil
2 T. vinegar or	1 t. chile powder
lemon juice	

Rub salad bowl with garlic. Dice avocado and place in bowl. Cut tomatoes in cubes and drain well. Chop radishes and onion; shred lettuce and combine with avocado. Add tomatoes. Blend olive oil, chile powder and vinegar and add to salad ingredients. Chill and serve.

Ensalada de Berro
Watercress Salad

Wash watercress carefully. Chop a small onion. Rub bowl with garlic. Combine ingredients, place in a bowl and serve with the following oil dressing:

8 T. olive oil	1 t. salt
4 T. vinegar or	1 t. sugar
lemon juice	1 t. chile powder
1 T. onion juice	1 T. tomato sauce

Put ingredients in a covered jar and shake thoroughly until well blended.

Ensalada de Col y Cebolla
Cabbage and Onion Salad

1 clove garlic	1 shredded onion
2 c. shredded cabbage	

Rub bowl with garlic. Combine cabbage and onion, place in bowl and mix with oil dressing.

ENSALADA DE FRIJOL
Bean Salad

2 c. cooked beans	½ small chopped onion
½ c. diced celery	2 T. prepared mustard
3 green chile peppers	6 T. cream or evaporated
2 medium chopped	milk
cucumber pickles	Salt
	Pepper

Combine all ingredients except mustard and cream. Beat mustard into cream and add to salad mixture. Serve on lettuce. Sprinkle with chile powder.

ENSALADA DE LECHUGA
Lettuce Salad

1 head lettuce	1 small chopped onion

SALSA
Dressing

1 clove garlic	1 t. chile powder
4 T. olive oil	Salt
2 T. vinegar	Pepper

Chop lettuce and add onion. Serve with the olive oil dressing which has been prepared at least 6 hours before using. To prepare dressing: Place olive oil and other ingredients in a covered jar. Shake well and leave until flavors are blended.

ENSALADA MEXICANA
Mexican Salad

2 large green sweet or	4 slices bacon
bell peppers	
1 medium onion	1 t. chile powder
4 medium ripe tomatoes	½ c. vinegar

Dice vegetables and mix. Cut bacon in squares and fry until crisp; stir in chile powder and add vinegar. As it boils pour over vegetables. Serve on lettuce leaves.

SOPAS
Soups

SOPA DE ALVERJONES
Pea Soup

1 c. dried peas	1 clove garlic
6 c. boiling water	2 t. salt
1 small onion sliced	1 T. fat

Cook peas with onion and garlic until done. Pass through colander using all liquid. Add salt and fat. Serve. *Garbanzo* (chick pea) or brown beans may be substituted for the peas in this recipe.

SOPA DE VERDURAS
Vegetable Soup

1 soup bone	1 red chile pod
6 c. water	1 clove garlic
1 c. green beans	1 t. dry mint
3 small squashes	2 t. salt
½ chopped onion	

Cook soup bone in water. When meat is cooked, strain soup. Add beans, squashes, onion, chile pod, and garlic to soup. Cook until beans are done. Add salt and mint. Serve.

PANES
Breads

BOLLITOS
Rolls

2 yeast cakes	1 t. salt
½ c. luke warm water	2 T. sugar
1½ c. milk	6 to 8 c. flour
4 T. fat	

Soak yeast in lukewarm water. Place milk in pan on top of stove. Add fat, salt, and sugar and leave until fat is melted. Cool to lukewarm. Add yeast, mixing well. Add flour, gradually, until a medium soft dough results. Knead lightly. Let rise until double in bulk. Form dough into balls, patting into round about 2½ inches in diameter. Fold in half. Place on a greased pan. Grease rolls on top. Let rise double in size. Bake in hot oven until brown on both sides.

Bizcocho
Toasted Rolls

Break rolls in half, place in a slow oven and toast until dry and crisp. Store to serve with *sopa* (soup) or as breakfast toast.

Bunuelos (Erroneously Called Sopaipillas)
Fried Bread

2 c. white flour	2 T. fat
2 c. whole wheat flour	1 c. water or enough to
1 t. salt	make medium soft dough
4 t. baking powder	4 c. lard substitute for frying

Sift flour, salt and baking powder together. Work fat into flour and add water. Knead well; let stand ½ hour. Form into flat balls and roll ⅛ inch thick in round shapes or cut in squares. Fry in deep fat until brown. Drain.

Molletes
Sweet Rolls

Make dough as for rolls and let rise. To this dough add 2 beaten eggs, 1 cup sugar, 2 t. anise seed, and 3 T. fat. Shape into round rolls. Let rise for 1 hour. Bake in hot oven. Slice and butter to serve with chocolate, coffee, or tea.

Tortillas de Trigo
Wheat Tortillas

2 c. white flour	1½ t. salt
2 c. whole wheat flour	3 T. fat
2 t. baking powder	1 c. water or enough to make medium dough

Sift flour, salt and baking powder together; add fat and mix well. Add water. Knead dough for 5 minutes. Let stand ½ hour covered. Form into round, flat balls and roll with rolling pin into a round shape about ⅛ inch thick. Cook on griddle on top of stove, or in the oven. Brown on both sides.

EMPAREDADOS
Sandwiches

EMPAREDADO DE AGUACATE
Avocado Sandwich

1 c. mashed avocados	1 t. salt
2 T. chopped green chile	4 T. grated cheese
1 T. catsup	1 t. chopped onion
2 drops of Tabasco sauce	Lettuce

Mash cheese; add avocado and other ingredients. Spread between slices of bread.

EMPAREDADO DE FRIJOL
Bean Sandwich

1 c. cooked beans	2 T. chopped sour pickles
2 T. finely chopped onion	1 T. prepared mustard
	Lettuce
2 T. chopped green chile	

Mash beans, add other ingredients, and spread on bread.

EMPAREDADO DE QUESO Y CHILE VERDE
Cheese and Green Chile Sandwich

Slice cheese thin to fit slice of bread. Cover with finely chopped green chile. Place under the broiler or in the oven and toast until cheese melts.

MACHITOS
Bean and Tortilla Sandwich

Spread a wheat or corn *tortilla* with leftover beans which have been seasoned with pork cracklings. Fold *tortilla* and serve.

Tacos are definitely a Mexican importation but the recipe given below is a New Mexican adaptation.

Tacos
Tortillas Filled with Meat

8 corn *tortillas*	1 T. parsley
1 lbs. of boiling meat	1 c. cooked diced potatoes
(pork or beef)	2 c. chile sauce (p. 47)
2 cloves chopped garlic	1 small onion
2 t. *orégano*	1 small head of lettuce

Prepare *tortillas*. Fry and fold in center, while frying. Cook meat and grind. Add seasonings, potatoes and chile. Boil until quite thick. Place meat mixture, diced onion and shredded lettuce between folded *tortillas*. Serve with chile sauce if desired.

POSTRES
Desserts

Arroz en Leche
Rice Pudding

1 c. rice	4 c. milk
5 c. water	1 c. sugar
1 t. salt	2 eggs
	Cinnamon

Wash rice thoroughly. Cook in boiling, salted water until it begins to swell. Drain. Add hot milk, stir in sugar and continue cooking until well done. Beat eggs and add to cooked rice. Cook 5 minutes. Serve in dessert dishes. Sprinkle top with cinnamon.

Calabaza al Horno — 1
Baked Pumpkin — 1

1 small pumpkin	1 t. cinnamon
1 c. sugar	1 t. salt

Remove seeds from pumpkin. Cut into 2-inch squares, leaving shell on. Place pieces in baking dish. Sprinkle with sugar, cinnamon and salt. Bake until pulp is soft. Serve in shell with boiled milk.

Baked Pumpkin — II

1 small pumpkin	1 t. salt
2 c. sugar	2 c. milk

Remove seeds from pumpkin. Peel and cut into 2-inch cubes. Place in baking dish. Sprinkle with sugar. Add milk. Cook in moderate oven until done. It may be necessary to add more milk to keep pumpkin from drying.

CAPIROTADA
Bread Pudding

1 c. sugar	1 t. cinnamon
2 c. water	1½ c. grated or sliced cheese
6 slices toasted bread	1 c. raisins
	2 T. fat

Caramelize sugar, add water and cinnamon, and boil until sugar is dissolved. Place a layer of bread in a casserole; add cheese and raisins. Repeat until all ingredients are used. Pour syrup over mixture, add fat and bake in moderate oven until the syrup is absorbed by the bread.

NATILLAS
Boiled Custard

4 c. milk	¾ c. sugar
4 eggs	½ t. salt
4 T. flour	Cinnamon

Heat the milk. Beat egg whites until stiff. Pour into hot milk, being careful that milk does not boil over. When egg whites are cooked, skim off from milk and place in a serving bowl. Mix flour, sugar, salt and beaten egg yolks; and add to hot milk. Cook for 10 minutes. Pour into egg whites and sprinkle top with cinnamon.

PANOCHA
Sprouted Wheat Pudding

The flour may be prepared at home or bought already prepared.
To sprout wheat, wash and drain, but do not dry. Place in a
cloth bag in a warm place to sprout. When the wheat has sprouted
(it takes 2 or 3 days), dry in sun. Grind into flour.

5 c. sprouted wheat flour	2 c. sugar (if desired)
2½ c. whole wheat flour	4 T. butter
7 c. boiling water or more for a soft consistency	

Mix the whole wheat and sprouted wheat flour thoroughly, add
one half the boiling water, and stir well. Set aside and cover. Let
stand for 15 minutes; then add the rest of the water. If sugar is
used, caramelize the sugar, add 1 cup of boiling water and when
sugar is dissolved, add to flour mixture. Boil mixture for 2 hours,
add butter and place uncovered in oven for 1 hour or until it is
quite thick and deep brown. Some people prefer to leave sugar out,
as the sprouted wheat has its own sugar.

TORREJAS ENMELADAS
Sweet Fritters

For making fritters see (p. 60.)

1 c. sugar	1 t. cinnamon
2 c. water	

Caramelize sugar. Add water and cinnamon. Boil until sugar
dissolves and syrup thickens. Drop egg fritters into syrup. Let stand
until the fritters are coated with sugar. Serve hot as dessert.

PASTAS
Pastries

BIZCOCHITOS
Sugar Cookies

1 c. sugar	2 c. whole wheat flour
2 c. shortening	1 t. salt
1 t. anise seed	2 t. baking powder
4 c. white flour	About ¾ c. water

Cream lard with hand; add sugar and beat until light and fluffy. Add anise seed and flour which has been sifted with salt and baking powder to the lard mixture. Add enough water to make the mixture hold together. Roll ½ inch thick and cut into fancy shapes. Dip in sugar and bake in a moderate oven.

EMPANADAS DE FRUTA
Fruit Turnovers

1½ c. flour	8 T. shortening
1 t. baking powder	4 to 6 T. water
1 t. salt	

Sift flour with baking powder and salt. Cut in shortening and mix well. Add enough water to make a dough easy to handle. Roll out dough ⅛ inch thick. Cut in rounds about 3 inches in diameter. Fill each round with fruit filling.

Fruit Filling

2 c. cooked dried fruit	1 t. cinnamon
1 c. sugar	½ t. cloves

Pass drained fruit through colander. (Canned, drained fruit may be used.) Add sugar and spices. Press edges of filled dough and pinch ends between thumb and forefinger, giving the dough half a turn. Bake in hot oven until brown.

EMPANADITAS DE CARNE
Meat Turnovers
Mincemeat

1 lb. boiling meat (cooked)	1 t. ground coriander seed
1½ c. raisins	½ t. cloves
2 c. apple sauce or jam	1 t. cinnamon
1 c. sugar	1 t. salt
	½ c. shelled piñón nuts

Grind meat, add raisins, apple sauce, sugar, nuts and spices. If the mixture is too dry, add a little of the meat stock but be careful that the paste is not soft. It should be moist but thick in consistency. Make dough for turnovers as follows:

1 cake yeast	1½ t. salt
1½ c. water or milk	2 T. sugar
3 T. fat	Flour

Soak yeast in warm water. Heat water or milk; add fat, salt and sugar. Cool to lukewarm and add dissolved yeast. Add enough flour to make a medium dough. Do not let rise. Roll out dough to ⅛ inch thick. Cut with biscuit cutter. If the dough rises after the rounds are cut, roll them thin. Place 1½ t. of mincemeat in center of rolled-out dough, fold and pinch together; then make a turn back in the dough taking edges between thumb and forefinger, pressing together and turning back in ridges.

Let turnovers stand for 5 minutes; then fry in deep fat until evenly browned.

MARQUESOTE
Sponge Cake

8 eggs	2 t. anise seed
1 c. pulverized sugar	10 T. cornstarch

Beat egg whites until stiff, add sugar and anise seed. Beat egg yolks and add corn starch. Add egg yolk mixture to egg whites mixture, beating constantly. Pour into greased cake pan to ½ full. Bake in moderate oven.

Sopaipillas
Sweet Fried Cakes

These are nice cakes for serving with chocolate or tea.

4 c. flour	4 eggs
1 t. salt	½ c. sugar
2 t. baking powder	Water or milk
4 t. fat	

Sift flour with salt and baking powder. Cut fat into flour. Beat eggs, add sugar, and add to flour mixture. Add enough milk or water to make a medium dough neither stiff nor soft. Let dough stand for ½ hour. Roll out ¼ inch thick, cut into 1½ inch squares and fry in deep fat until brown.

To ½ cup of sugar add 2 teaspoons cinnamon and mix well. As the *sopaipillas* are fried and drained and still hot, roll in the sugar and cinnamon mixture.

Enmeladas
Fried Cakes in Syrup

Make *sopaipillas* as in above recipe. After they have been fried dip into syrup.

Syrup

6 c. sugar	1 t. cinnamon
3 c. water	

Caramelize sugar. When melted and brown add water. Cook until thick. Add cinnamon, mixing well. Each *sopaipilla* is dipped separately into the syrup and taken out immediately. Drain on platter. Serve as dessert.

BEBIDAS
Beverages

Most of the recipes given here are for drinks usually served to sick or old people, or to children. They are light, nutritious foods.

ATOLE
Cornmeal Gruel

½ c. blue cornmeal   2½ c. boiling water

Stir cornmeal in ½ c. water, add to boiling water. Boil until it has reached the consistency of cream. Serve in cups about half full. Add enough salted boiled milk to fill cups. This is a very common beverage for sick or old people.

CAFÉ CON LECHE
Coffee with Milk

Make coffee good and strong. Heat milk to boiling (goat's milk preferred). Fill coffee cups ¼ full with hot milk. Fill with coffee and serve.

CHOCOLATE
Chocolate

1 qt. milk   ½ c. boiling water
1 inch stick cinnamon   ½ t. vanilla
3 T. strong coffee   ⅛ t. salt
2 squares sweet chocolate ½ t. nutmeg
   or 4 T. cocoa

Heat milk to boiling with cinnamon and coffee. Remove cinnamon and add chocolate dissolved in boiling water. Heat again to boiling. Remove from fire, and add vanilla, nutmeg and salt. Beat with egg beater or *molinillo* (chocolate beater) until foamy. If commercially prepared spiced chocolate is used, proceed as follows: To 1 qt. of milk add 2 squares of chocolate dissolved in 1 c. boiling water. Keep over fire until it comes to a boil. Beat with egg beater or chocolate beater. (4 T. cocoa may be substituted for chocolate. If this is done add 1 t. butter.)

PINOLE
Corn Meal Drink

4 T. corn meal	1 c. milk
½ t. cinnamon	2 T. maple sugar

Mix corn meal with cinnamon. Stir into cold milk, and add sugar. Stir well and serve. If maple sugar is not available, use ½ t. maple flavoring and 2 T. white sugar. To be palatable the corn meal must be made from toasted corn. In New Mexico, the native corn meal is always ground from toasted corn.

POLVILLO
Toasted Flour Gruel

Toast wheat flour in oven until brown. Stir constantly while browning or it will scorch. Any amount may be browned for it will keep indefinitely if kept in a jar covered with cheese cloth.

6 T. browned flour	2 c. boiling water
4 t. cold water	White, brown or maple sugar

Dissolve flour in cold water, pour into boiling water and cook thoroughly. Sweeten with sugar to taste.

MISCELLANEOUS

Cocktail de Aguacate
Avocado Cocktail

Select 4 small avocados which are firm, cut into small squares (about ¼ inch). Prepare sauce as follows: 1 c. catsup, 1 c. diced celery, 2 T. lemon juice, or 1 T. vinegar, 4 drops Tabasco sauce, 1 t. salt, 1 t. sugar. Serve avocados in cocktail glasses and put 2 T. of the prepared sauce in each serving. (Serves 12)

Cocktail de Camarón
Shrimp Cocktail

3 T. catsup	½ t. red chile powder or 2 drops Tabasco sauce
3 T. chopped celery	1 T. Worcestershire sauce
1 T. lemon juice	½ t. salt

Mix all ingredients thoroughly. Place canned or fresh shrimp in cocktail glasses. Add 1 T. of the sauce for each serving. Top with an olive.

Cocktail de Jugo de Tomates
Tomato Juice Cocktail

2 c. tomato juice	1 T. onion juice
1 t. salt	½ t. red chile powder
⅛ t. celery salt	1 T. lemon juice

Boil tomato juice with spices and onion. Strain and cool. Add lemon juice. Serve in glasses and top with a sprig of mint.

GLOSSARY

9

The words in this glossary may have other meanings, but the one given here explains the meaning as used in this composition.

Adobo — *A preparation for curing meat*
Aguinaldos — *Christmas gifts*
Aleluyas — *A religious sect commonly called "Holy Rollers"*
Amole — *Soap weed — root of yucca plant*
Azafrán — *Saffron — Crocus sativus*
Bizcochitos — *Sugar cookies*
Buñuelos — *Fried bread*
Cabrito — *Young goat*
Canaigre — *Wild pieplant — Rumex hymenosepalus*
Capilla — *Small church*
Capirotada — *A bread pudding*
Cáscara de capulín — *Choke cherry bark — Prunus melanocarpa*
Castilleja — *Beard tongue or paintbrush — Castilleja hololeuca*
Chicos — *Dried steamed green corn*
Chamiza — *Atriplex canescens*
Chimajá — *Wild parsley — Aulospermum purpureum*
Contrahierba — *Dorstenia contrayerba*
Coto — *Galium — an herb of the madder family*

Comadre — *Co-mother* — *Relation between godmother and the real mother*
Curandera — *Medicine woman*
Despensa — *Store room* — *pantry*
Dolientes — *Mourners*
Doña — *Mistress* — *lady*
Donas — *Trousseau*
Empanaditas — *Fried turnovers*
Entrega — *Presentation of newlyweds to their parents*
Espinacito — *Spinal cord (diminutive)*
Estafiata — *Wormwood* — *Artemisia frigida*
Feliz Navidad — *Merry Christmas*
Guisado — *Plainly cooked and then seasoned*
Harinilla — *Meal ground from lime hominy*
Hasta mañana — *Until tomorrow*
Hediondilla — *Creosote* — *Covillea tridendata*
Hoguera — *Bonfire*
Inmortal — *Spider milkweed* — *Asclepiodora decumbens*
Jesús y Cruz — *Invocation to Jesus*
Malvas — *Common mallow* — *Malva rotundifolia*
Mariola — *Rubber bush* — *Parthenium incannum*
Marquesotes — *Sponge cakes*
Masa — *Dough for bread or for tamales*
Manzanilla — *Camomile* — *Anthemis nobilis*
Mastranzo — *Round leaved mint* — *Mentha rotundifolia*
Meneador — *Stick used for stirring*
Memoria — *A puzzle ring given as a remembrance*
Molletes — *Sweet rolls*
Morcilla — *Blood sausage*
Muy buenas noches — *Goodnight*
Nixtamal — *Lime hominy*
Orégano — *Horse mint* — *Monardella lanceolata*
Oshá — *Wild mountain parsnip, loveroot* — *Ligusticum porteri*
Padrinos — *Best man and bride's maid*
Panocha — *Cereal made from sprouted wheat flour*
Patrón — *Master*
Piñón — *Small nuts from the piñón tree (Pinus edulus)*

Poleo — *Pennyroyal* — *Mentha pulegium*
Poñil — *Apache Plume* — *Fallugia paradoxa*
Pozole — *Stew made from lime hominy*
Prendorio — *Betrothal feast*
Quelites — *Lambs' quarters* — *Chenopodium album*
Rezador — *One who leads the prayers*
Ristras — *Strings of chile*
Sala — *A large room — a living room — also applied to a dance hall*
Señá — *Dialectic for señora*
Tequesquite — *A sodium nitrate commonly used in colonial times
    in place of today's baking powder*
Tortillas — *Flat round bread*
Torrejas — *Fritters*
Verdolagas — *Purslane* — *Portulaca oleracea cleome*
Waco — *Bee weed* — *Peritoma serrulata*
Yerba de la Negrita — *Bristly mallow (Modiola Caroliniana)
    Malvacea*
Yerba de la víbora — *Snake brush* — *Gutierrezia*

MORNING SONG

Ya viene el alba	Daylight breaks
Ya viene el día	The dawn is here
Cantemos todos	Let us all sing
Ave María	Ave Maria

CHRISTMAS HYMN

Oremus, Oremus	Let us pray, Let us pray
Angelitos somos	Angels from heaven are we
Del cielo venimos	Asking for gifts in His name
A pedir Aguinaldos y oremus	Please do not turn us away

WEDDING ADAGE

Martes ni te cases ni te embarques.
Tuesday neither wed nor embark.

INDEX

10

86

89

95